ALSO BY MAG(

The Busy Person's Guide To Energy Clearing

The Busy Person's Guide To Space Clearing

The Busy Person's Guide To Ghosts, Curses & Aliens

The Busy Person's Guide: The Complete Series on Energy Clearing

The Nature of Intuition: Understand & Harness Your Intuitive Ability

Caring For Your Animal Companion: The Intuitive, Natural Way To A Happy, Healthy Pet

Dowsing Ethics: Replacing Intentions With Integrity

The Practical Pendulum Series, Volumes 1-4

Pendulum Proficiency: You Can Learn To Dowse

How To Dowse Accurately & With Confidence

Dowsing Pitfalls & Protection

Dowse Your Way To Health: An Introduction To Health Dowsing

Dowsing: Practical Enlightenment

101 Amazing Things You Can Do With Dowsing

Ask The Right Question: The Essential Sourcebook Of Good Dowsing Questions

The Dowsing Encyclopedia

The Essence Of Dowsing by Nigel Percy

The Credibility Of Dowsing, edited by Nigel Percy

Healing Made Simple: Change Your Mind & Improve Your Health

Dowsing Box Set

Dowsing Reference Library

Space Clearing: Beyond Feng Shui

Visit Sixth Sense Books (www.sixthsensebooks.com) to see all our books, to get notification of new releases and for links to our fiction author sites.

THE DOWSING STATE

SECRET KEY TO ACCURATE DOWSING

MAGGIE PERCY
NIGEL PERCY

Cover by: Zoran Petrovic, Fiverr name Visual Arts

ISBN: 978-1-946014-19-1 (Ebook edition)

ISBN: 978-1-946014-20-7 (Paperback edition)

Sixth Sense Books

150 Buck Run E

Dahlonega, GA 30533

www.sixthsensebooks.com

CONTENTS

PREFACE

What if it were possible to focus your intuition and get answers to questions you can't answer rationally? Well, it is! The skill of dowsing is a natural technique anyone can learn, and it allows you to 'know' things your rational mind cannot know. But instead of waiting for a hunch or intuitive hit to come unbidden out of nowhere, you can reach inside using dowsing and get the answers you seek.

The way you focus your intuition is through an altered state called simply 'the dowsing state.' It is measurably different in terms of your brain wave patterns from any other state: resting, sleeping, dreaming, meditating. The dowsing state has not been studied a lot, nor has it been scientifically explained, but one thing is known: if you aren't in a dowsing state, you can't really dowse. Your answers won't be any more accurate than guessing would yield.

The dowsing state is therefore the key to accurate dowsing. More than any other aspect, even more than asking a good question, the dowsing state allows you to get answers that are meaningful.

The dowsing state is hard to describe and even harder to teach, so in the past, many courses didn't even bother. This terrible lack led to people thinking that dowsing was just being able to get a yes/no response with a tool. It also caused people to feel training was unnecessary. They regarded dowsing as a psychic ability instead of a skill. Many came to regard it as a joke, because they couldn't get accurate answers. Dowsing became like the ouija board: a shiny thing that arouses curiosity, but is just a parlor trick in the hands of amateurs.

In this book, we show you more about the dowsing state than you've ever seen in any class, yet there is still so much we don't understand about it. Science is not capable of measuring and explaining much about the dowsing process at this time. One day, it may be.

Until then, it's important not to lose sight of the vital nature of the dowsing state in the process of dowsing. The dowsing state is your gateway to focused intuition. It's like the wormhole to the place with all the answers. Without the key to that wormhole, you can't get there. You can't get answers. You can't be a good dowser.

For most dowsers, the dowsing state is like making a good question: the boring part you want to rush past so you can do the actual dowsing. But like asking a good question, being in a proper dowsing state is your only hope for getting an accurate answer, so it is important that you are able to get into a dowsing state every time you dowse. This book will help you understand what this altered state is, what it does and how you can achieve it. We want to help you become the best dowser you can be.

One final comment: In speaking about dowsing and the dowsing state, we are passionate and opinionated; our opinions are based on years of experience, but they are not fixed—they continue to evolve with new evidence, experience and arguments. While we disagree with certain views and approaches, we believe that all dowsers have good intentions and love dowsing, so any opinion we offer is about a belief, protocol or approach; it is not a personal attack.

We believe debate and discussion is an important aspect of progress and learning, so we encourage you to engage your critical thinking skills with an open mind and judge for yourself the logic of what we say. Then test it and see how it works for you. We all continue to learn by following this practice.

We realize that our point of view does not resonate with everyone and in some cases may contradict what you have been taught or assumed was true. We trust that you will use your natural intelligence and curiosity to examine the details of what we say and test them for efficacy rather than rejecting them outright. Sometimes a new way of looking at something is the key that opens the door to success.

Maggie Percy

August 1, 2017

ACKNOWLEDGMENTS

I want to express appreciation to Ed Stillman for his excellent research, without which this book would lack a great deal of credibility. While I make it clear that I believe we should not wait for science to conclude that dowsing is a real activity that yields actual results, it is wonderful to have scientific methods confirm what masterful dowsers already know: that dowsing works, that is something totally different from using the rational mind and physical senses, and that dowsing well and regularly creates changes in how you see the world and interact with it.

I tried to contact Ed while I wrote this book, hoping I could interview him or maybe get him to review the manuscript before I published, but we were unable to connect. Any errors made in the summary of Ed's work are entirely my own.

A heartfelt thanks also goes out to the members of the Dowsing Tribe who responded to my request for their perception of and experience with the dowsing state. I received tons of replies that helped shape this book into a tool that I hope will expand the dowsing horizons of those who read it. I wish I could name each and every person who took the time to respond to my questions, sharing their experiences generously and bravely admitting in many cases that they didn't know about the dowsing state or had problems accessing it, but there are too many to list. Please accept my gratitude for your assistance.

Maggie Percy

July, 2017

1

BEFORE YOU START

How To Get The Most Out Of This Book

Life is busy, and we all want sound bites instead of having to take the time to read, think and process information. But if you want to learn about the dowsing state, there are no short cuts.

The dowsing state is a subtle, hard-to-describe process that good dowsers reach in order to get accurate answers, and it's a real bear to teach. There are many paths to reaching a dowsing state. There is no one-size-fits-all answer or method of doing it. For that reason, we implore you to read this book from cover to cover. Then think about what it says and tune in to your intuition and employ the suggestions that most resonate with you. We believe that in doing that, you will shorten your learning curve considerably.

Don't skip right to the chapter on "How To Get Into A Dowsing State." You need the background of the previous chapters to get the most out of it. A tendency to skip things here will leave you confused at best and at worst mean that you still can't get into a dowsing state or trust your dowsing answers.

As we state repeatedly throughout the book, you are not really dowsing if you are not in a dowsing state. Our surveys show that most dowsers, the vast majority in fact, either don't know about the dowsing state or have difficulty achieving it. Even veteran dowsers report inconsistent success with entering the dowsing state. If you read this book carefully and apply what we suggest, you will not only have a much better grasp of what the dowsing state is; you will be able to practice getting into it and learn how your body senses this altered state that is the gateway to a higher level of consciousness.

Our goal is to help you to be the best dowser you want to be. This book provides you with fundamental information that, if applied and practiced, will boost your dowsing results. Happy Dowsing!

2

THE MAGIC OF DOWSING

What Is The Magic Of Dowsing?

Many dowsing classes are taught poorly. The teachers spend most of their time on how to use dowsing tools, and little or none on how to get into a dowsing state or ask a good question. They have missed the point about dowsing. To them, dowsing is like magic, and the tool is a magic wand, so they want to spend all their time on the wand. But everyone knows that magic isn't real; that magicians thrive on misdirection. They know that the real 'magic' isn't in the wand; it is taking place where you can't see it. The same is true of dowsing.

The fact is this: you can master any esoteric technique for healing, for knowing, for being, but there is always a lot more to it than saying 'abracadabra' and waving a wand. The biggest part takes place within you, and that requires change. Anyone can learn to dowse, but you must invest time, effort and, yes, money to become a masterful dowser. And even if you make this commitment, it is unlikely that you will master more than a few specialties in the vast array of dowsing applications during your lifetime.

Each dowsing specialty has its own vocabulary, pitfalls, tricks and techniques. To master an application takes years. The average person, even the average dowser, doesn't realize this. They think if you can get a yes/no response, you can dowse about anything and expect correct answers. That's wrong, but most people don't bother researching to find out the truth. It's easier and more fun to think of dowsing as magic or a psychic talent.

Since you're reading this book, you have an interest in understanding dowsing and becoming masterful. The dowsing state is a vital factor in dowsing mastery. No, let's restate that. If you aren't in the dowsing state, you're not dowsing, so you darn well better learn how to access the dowsing state.

We've written a lot of books about dowsing. This one is perhaps the most esoteric of all. It talks about theory, technique and things that cannot be proven, yet are critical to successful dowsing. If you get through this book and apply what you have learned, your dowsing will improve. Of that we are certain.

The dowsing state is the most challenging aspect of dowsing to teach and learn. It is hard to describe. It is difficult at first to tell if you are in a dowsing state or not. Most of the so-called basic dowsing courses ignore this fact, and they churn out students who cannot dowse, because they haven't learned anything about the dowsing state.

The dowsing state is the true magic of dowsing. You don't change color or look different when you are in a dowsing state, but without it, you aren't dowsing. It's easier to show how tools move to indicate yes/no answers, but that is bypassing the important stuff, the stuff that takes time to experience, describe and master. You can learn how to use a tool in one short class or even a simple demo, but that isn't dowsing.

Even though the dowsing state is the very essence of dowsing, it's pretty ambitious to write a book about it, especially since most classes don't even talk about it. One would expect that very few people will be interested in reading this book. And that might be true. Most people get attracted to the shininess of something: the idea of writing a book, the thought of learning how to play a musical instrument, the dream of running a marathon. People join groups, buy courses and then put them aside and never do anything. The same is true of all subjects. Dowsing just happens to be one of the few we never put aside.

We are passionate about dowsing, even though we first learned it years ago. Our passion and our ability to see the potential in dowsing, the way it could change our lives, fueled our interest and drove us to invest time, effort and money in mastering it. Now, standing on the top of the mountain (or maybe only a very high hill), we see how few people have climbed to the top with us.

The road to mastery is not short. It is not easy. Few make it to the top. If you are reading this book, you have a spark of true interest in the real magic of dowsing. We will share all we know with you on this subject. There will be many unanswered questions at the end, but you will know far more than the average dowser ever learns. It will serve you in your quest for mastery.

You can't master dowsing just by reading a book or two. But if you read a dozen or two dozen and take a dozen courses or more and attend regular events that are high quality, and if you practice regularly, you will be among the few masterful dowsers in your particular area of dowsing interest. We have written this book to help you with that goal, because the dowsing state is the real magic of dowsing.

3

WHAT IS DOWSING?

How Do You Define Dowsing?

Back when we learned to dowse in the 1990s, everyone who knew about dowsing pretty much agreed on what it is. Historically, dowsing has most often been used in 'modern' times for finding water and minerals, but that is an application, not a definition of what dowsing is. Dowsing is basically a search for answers. You ask a question, and you get an answer. Water dowsing is the best known application of dowsing, where the dowser asks a question which can be summarized as, "Where's the water?".

There are many applications for this versatile skill. Anything that you want to know about, you ask questions about. And dowsing can give you answers. But it's more specific than that. Dowsing is an intuitive method for getting answers to questions you cannot answer rationally. After all, if you can find the answer on Google, why would you waste time dowsing?

In spite of the fact that dowsing is so versatile, it was only in the last several decades that people began to expand into other dowsing applications beyond finding water and minerals. Because dowsing has been called a psychic skill, most of the people who participated in expanding dowsing horizons were of the New Age mentality. They were interested in metaphysics, 'energies' and the invisible realm. They loved empowering techniques that were a bit 'woo-woo.' They adopted dowsing without much thought as to whether it is a psychic ability or not, without inspecting the process itself, without questioning whether it was a natural ability or not. Dowsing to them seemed like magic. It opened doors to other realms beyond the physical. They weren't that interested in examining the process or explaining it in detail. They weren't even that interested in practical applications or improving their lives with dowsing. They just wanted to play with it.

In these things they were, in a sense, the antithesis of water dowsers, who tend to be practical, grounded and focused on measurable results in the physical world. Yet, contrary to what you will hear from some people, all dowsers are always doing the same thing. They are asking questions and getting answers. It is a fallacy to see water or mineral dowsing as fundamentally different from energy dowsing. They are merely different applications of the same technique.

In spite of the 'woo-woo' beginnings of 'spiritual dowsing,' people began to see the value of adding dowsing to their healing practice or to clearing noxious environmental energies, because it enhanced the knowledge they had. They also realized they could use it to predict the future. By the late 90s, a wide variety of dowsing applications were being explored. But even amongst the ranks of the major national dowsing organizations, not a whole lot was being done to examine what dowsing really is and how best to teach it. Too many people still accepted it as a psychic ability rather than a skill. They adopted the idea of dowsing as magic that one could learn overnight. Or else they trained people as if they were dowsing for water, which didn't translate well into other dowsing applications. For years that approach was used by the American Society of Dowsers in its basic courses. We know, because we participated in many ASD events as teachers and presenters.

As the 21st century started, people were dowsing about all kinds of subjects and still understood that dowsing was about asking questions and getting answers. But the lack of rigor in training and the paucity of critical thinking and discussion about what dowsing really was meant that dowsing was an activity built on a foundation of sand. People didn't really understand what dowsing was. Some thought it was modern magic; some thought it was psychic ability; a few thought it was a natural skill.

As the interest in the world of energy and metaphysics grew, practitioners of dowsing, some of whom had little or no training, became 'gurus' who shared their viewpoint with the world. The ability to easily self-publish led to the proliferation of books on dowsing by people who weren't experts. Some of these 'gurus' became successful and gathered quite a following. Those who were most successful appeared to be in the camp of 'dowsing as magic' rather than 'dowsing as a natural skill.'

At first, this didn't seem to be such a bad thing. Everyone is entitled to their opinion. And it's pretty obvious that selling the sizzle is always good marketing. But years later, it is obvious that the emperor has no clothes. The dowsing community, once a moderately cohesive group of individuals who could all explain dowsing and agreed on the basics, is now fragmented, confused and even argumentative.

There are those who want to call dowsing a healing method, which it is not. There are those who want to call the use of intention 'dowsing' if you are holding a pendulum at the time. That is not dowsing, either. Yet, because of the sexiness of the 'silver bullet' style of those methods, they caught on. And because of the cult of personality surrounding some dowsing 'gurus,' you cannot question certain things without starting a riot. Dowsing has in effect been turned into a religion. You aren't allowed to think, nor are you allowed to question dogma. This has stifled meaningful discussion.

Yet, the 'new' view of dowsing, the totally transformed image of dowsing as a healing method or a way to transform energies, hasn't really caught on, either. While there are plenty of people who define dowsing that way, almost none of them really uses it for any practical application. The reason for that is that no one is training anyone to use it successfully. Their style of dowsing is all based on faith rather than training. So people get tired of using it, because they don't get results. In spite of their lack of results, they aren't interested in training, because they have been brainwashed into thinking they don't need it.

There are some people who are interested in learning about dowsing and how to use it to change their lives. You are among them. Those people who are willing to think, to question and to learn will be the next generation of real dowsers. They will know that dowsing is a natural intuitive skill that complements rational thought as a way of getting answers to questions. They understand that the rational mind has limitations.

Intuition offers a complementary array of sensing abilities to enhance your results in life. Dowsing engages those abilities, as it is a skill you can master that will tap into answers you can't get using your rational mind. Instead of waiting around for an intuitive hit or gut feeling, you can dowse right here, right now and get answers. Dowsing focuses your intuition. This makes you a more intelligent being and gives you an increased chance of success in life. But it is a skill and requires training and practice, and that is where we try to help people.

Dowsing is a priceless tool for improving your life. It isn't magic. It isn't a psychic ability. It's a part of being human. The New Agers who first expanded the use of dowsing didn't see it that way, and all subsequent activity was colored by the mistaken impressions and assumptions mentioned above. Starting over with a clean slate, dowsers will be able to see that dowsing is a part of being fully human. It will probably still remain an esoteric practice, because it demands a level of commitment that most people aren't willing to invest. But that does not mean it is given only to a few, special people. Anyone who reaches for it can succeed in mastering it.

. . .

What Are The Key Elements Of Dowsing?

There is much confusion these days about what dowsing is. While dowsing is not in itself a healing method, it is a valuable tool for healers. In spite of dowsing not being an energy transformation tool, dowsing has been priceless to us as we transform energies on our path.

Now that you know the definition of dowsing, it will be helpful to identify the key elements of the dowsing process. In other words, if you leave all the shiny stuff out, what are the essential parts of the dowsing process, the things without which you cannot dowse?

They are:

1. A goal

2. A good dowsing question

3. The dowsing state

4. Dowsing the question

5. Getting the answer

6. As often as possible, confirming the answer

We'll go into details on all these aspects shortly, but first let's point out that intention is not part of the dowsing process. Healing is not part of the dowsing process. Energy transformation is not part of the dowsing process. You don't see a tool listed. In spite of the emphasis on tools in dowsing classes, they are not required for dowsing. In fact, in a later section, we'll talk about the results of a scientific study that suggests that deviceless dowsing is perhaps a better way to dowse, and why.

Let's examine the items in the list of key parts of the dowsing process.

Number 1: Having a goal

This is totally ignored by most dowsers and teachers. If you don't have a goal, and if you aren't clear what that goal is, you will never be able to make a good dowsing question.

You dowse for a reason. Dowsing is a search for an answer, an answer that you feel is going to somehow make your life better. Dowsing is not intended for frivolous activities or parlor tricks. It's a tool for your life. As such, it's important to know what your goal is before you dowse. Taking the time to think about what your goal is will set you up for making a good dowsing question. It may seem obvious, but most people do not stop to ask why they are dowsing. What is their reason for asking the question? Without clear goals, you cannot dowse well.

Another advantage to thinking about your goal is that this is the step in the process where you need to check in with your dowsing ethics. Just because you can dowse doesn't mean you should dowse. If you think about your goal, you will also be able to reflect on whether you are invading someone's privacy or doing something out of ego. So this is a very important step in the process.

Number 2: A good dowsing question

Another subject that is rarely taught in dowsing courses (and if it is taught, it is taught badly or lacking in depth), is the essential nature of asking a good question. Even those who pay lip service to this topic rarely know how to ask a good question. Yet, if your question is not good, your answer will be useless.

Time and again we see how weak people are in asking a good dowsing question. This is in part due to the tendency to rush to get the answer. But it is also partially due to a reluctance to use the rational faculty or the doubt that they are capable of forming a good question.

Dowsing is a brain balancing activity, because to be a good dowser, you must use both sides of your brain. Making a good dowsing question is a left brain or rational activity. Those who mistrust the rational mind or prefer intuition may try to sidestep this part of the process, which sabotages results.

Even if you are not strong in terms of left brain activities, you can learn to ask a good dowsing question. Our book on asking a good question is available at Sixth Sense Books, www.sixthsensebooks.com and all major online retailers. Every real dowser needs to have and use a copy of *Ask The Right Question*. It is the most comprehensive book on the subject and the fact that it is our best-selling book for dowsers proves the need for what it contains.

Number 3: The dowsing state

Without the dowsing state, which is rarely taught in courses, you are not dowsing. Anyone can grab a pendulum and get a yes/no response. You can get an answer from your tool without being in a dowsing state, because the tool is merely amplifying subtle physical reactions of your body to the question. In a sense, you are indeed making the tool move. However, the movement of a tool and the reaction of your body when in the dowsing state is real, while the tool moving when you are not in the dowsing state is an artifact and not to be trusted.

The purpose of this book is to examine this particular step in the dowsing process. We want you to be aware of what the other key steps are. Without all of them, you won't be an accurate dowser. Our other books and courses cover the other steps in the process, so we won't be going into detail about them here.

Number 4: Dowsing the question

You must be in a dowsing state to do this, and it is the core of good dowsing. If you have numbers 1-3 mastered, this part isn't that difficult, but it takes practice. Some detail on this step will be covered in this book.

. . .

NUMBER 5: Getting the answer

This is the shortest but most rewarding part of the process. If you have done the first four steps well, your answer will be more accurate. Most novices make the mistake of jumping straight to this step. You cannot dowse accurately if you do that. Since the requirements for getting an answer complement the requirements for being in a dowsing state, we will address this step in more detail later.

NUMBER 6: Confirming the answer

Most courses leave out this key part of the process. If you cannot confirm your answer is right, how can you be sure you are a good dowser? Obviously, you cannot. Yet many people claim to be good dowsers who rarely, if ever, dowse about subjects they can confirm.

When we mention confirming answers, we aren't talking about coin tosses and card suits or fake tests of your dowsing ability. We refer to everyday dowsing about subjects you want or need to know about and cannot answer rationally, which you can later confirm. About 80% of your dowsing should be this type of dowsing if you hope to master the skill. Get our book *101 Amazing Things You Can Do With Dowsing* for loads of ideas of what to dowse about to improve your skill.

CAN ANYONE LEARN TO DOWSE?

Because dowsing is often listed as a psychic activity, most people don't believe they can learn to dowse, or dowse well. They don't see themselves as psychics. They are amazed when they get a yes/no response with their tool. We cannot state this strongly enough: dowsing is not a psychic ability. It is not something that you have fully developed when you are born. It is a skill, and as a skill, it requires training and practice to master.

People are always looking for a silver bullet. It's a natural human trait. We all want quick answers. But skills cannot be mastered quickly. That is why most people refuse to see dowsing as a skill. They would rather think it is a magical or psychic ability, because they can convince themselves that they might be able to quickly master it if that is the case. The people who delude themselves this way never become good dowsers. There are no short cuts to mastery.

Dowsing is a natural human ability that allows you to focus your intuition. You can get answers to questions you cannot answer rationally. But your accuracy will depend on your level of skill. Anyone can dowse. Almost anyone can master dowsing. But to master dowsing, you must invest time and effort in learning the skill and practicing it. As with any skill, some will find mastery easier than others; some will seem to have a natural talent for certain types of dowsing.

Sadly, due to the way it is perceived and taught, most people don't see the value in dowsing. That is a real shame, because dowsing can save your life or save you a ton of money. It can help you make good decisions about where to live, whom to marry and what career to choose. Dowsing is a priceless skill, and if you decide to master it, your life will never be the same. Dowsing is even valuable for reducing everyday stress (a major cause of disease) by helping you make good choices on small decisions that otherwise would create worry and fear.

Dowsing is like any type of esoteric knowledge, whether that knowledge is about healing or martial arts or enlightenment. The path to mastery is long and arduous. You can learn to become an accurate dowser. It will take time and effort. Be patient with yourself. Just keep working at it. The results will repay you a hundredfold.

4

WHAT IS THE DOWSING STATE & WHY DO YOU NEED IT?

Connecting To Answers

When you want to make a phone call to a friend and ask her to join you for dinner, you need to have a connection in order to find out her answer. If you are using a landline, the connection is signaled by the dial tone. If there is no dial tone, you cannot make the call. Similarly, if you use a cell phone, and there are no bars on your phone, you cannot connect with your friend and get her answer.

You know the goal you have in mind. You know you want to find out if your friend can dine with you tomorrow night. But the only way you can get an answer is to talk with her, and she is not conveniently located. So the phone is your best bet. Alternatively, you may reach out to her via email. But if your internet connection is down, that will not work. In other words, to communicate over distance requires a connection of some type for the question or message to go through and for the answer to come back.

Think of dowsing as a type of communication or connection via which you get information to answer a question you have, a question that cannot be answered in other ways. If you cannot get a connection, you won't be able to get an answer.

The dowsing state is that connection. It is that open line that allows the question to go out from you and the answer to return to you. It isn't easy at first to tell if you have the open line of communication that will allow the answer to come through.

Imagine if your phone did not give a dial tone to show you could dial a number. If you picked up the phone, and if you didn't get the dial tone, what would you do? You'd probably stop and wonder if the phone was working. That would be pretty frustrating and not easy to adapt to, because you wouldn't be getting reinforcement for right action. We expect outward stimuli to indicate we are going in the right direction. With dowsing, the stimuli are subtle and internal, and in most cases, they are things you haven't been taught to notice or pay attention to. So you have trouble knowing if you are in the dowsing state, especially as a newbie.

With dowsing, as with the phone call, there is a strong desire to get an answer, to have a connection. We have repeatedly seen that the expectation of getting a "yes" or "no" answer in dowsing leads to the motion of the tool, whether the person is in a dowsing state or not. The small amount of response the body needs in order to make the tool move is easily given by a strong expectation of a response.

Novice dowsers lack practice in detachment and most of the time have not disconnected from their rational faculties, and they end up getting the answer they expect. But that isn't dowsing. It's almost like they're hearing voices that are not there...filling in the silence, because at some level, they know there is no connection. The human need for positive reinforcement overcomes patience, and people think they are getting responses just because they want them. And there is no easy way to tell the difference between a real dowsing response and a false one.

It's too bad that you don't get a signal like a dial tone that lets you know you have reached the dowsing state, so you can proceed to ask your question. We have been so programmed in physical reality to rely on outside stimuli that we do not have the training or experience to notice intuitive reactions. We allow our emotions and wishful thinking, both quite strong, to speak louder than our Inner Voice. If you wish to learn to dowse, you will have to discard these tendencies and cultivate new habits so that you can 'hear' your intuition.

People who have been trained to listen to their Inner Voice, or even just trained to be comfortable with silence, as in meditation, seem to have an advantage for learning about the dowsing state. This fact would also seem to make it slightly advantageous to be introverted, as introverts seem to be a bit more comfortable with silence than extroverts. And it would also seem likely that anyone with a monkey mind is going to have a disadvantage over someone who finds it easy to still her mental activity. Those who are inclined to multi-task will be at a disadvantage for the same reason. Dowsing is not something you do while you think about other things. You need to focus and empty the mind.

So the first requirement for the dowsing state is that you are opening a channel of silence so that your question can go out and the answer can come back to you. This is NOT channeling in the usual sense. It is just the decision to open a line of communication, to be open to hearing answers and not providing them yourself or guessing what they may be.

Where Do The Answers Come From?

Your next question may be, if I get into a dowsing state and get an answer, where is the answer coming from? While this is not strictly speaking a part of the dowsing state, it is a legitimate question. Your attitude about where the answers come from can affect your dowsing ability and accuracy as well as your attitude and understanding of dowsing.

There are many theories about where the answers come from when you dowse, and none of them can be proven. Some of the popular ones include:

•The Akashic Records/Library, which is more commonly used when referring to past lives

•One or more advanced beings, including God

•The "Field," an energetic repository of everything that has happened or will happen

There are any number of theories you can read about, but since none of them can be proven, it is up to you to use your judgment. We personally do not subscribe to the idea that dowsing is making a phone call to God or an advanced being. That would be channeling. Channeling is an activity best undertaken by someone who has had proper training. It is impossible to be a good channel without clearing a lot of your own 'stuff,' which would explain the appalling lack of sense, integrity and usefulness in channeled information you find on the internet. Most of it is utter tripe, because channeling is a skill that, like dowsing, requires training and practice and a great deal of self-work, and most people do not do those things. Channeling is also potentially a dangerous activity in addition to being pretty useless unless you have trained in how to do it well.

That leaves various types of energetic repositories or imprints or fields as the potential location of the answers to your dowsing questions. Since most of us now agree that everything is energy in some form, those explanations are pretty easy to believe. Unfortunately, they cannot be proven. Fortunately for you and us, it doesn't really matter exactly where the answers are located.

Our personal viewpoint is that dowsing is only empowering when you accept the responsibility and power for getting the answers yourself. We don't see dowsing as going to Teacher and asking the right answer to a question. That is not an empowering attitude, and that is not how we regard dowsing. We feel that dowsing is a turning inward for answers. We are connected to everything. We are a part of the great energy Universe. Everything 'out there' is a reflection of our own energy and beliefs. So when we dowse, we see it as looking inward for answers. That does not mean we believe the answers are within us physically, but that due to our connection to everything, we can find the answers by looking inward better than by looking outward. Looking outward is like trying to use a mirror to navigate. The outer world is a reflection of our inner selves, so the truest answers will come by looking inward, not outward.

When you are getting into a dowsing state, you merely need to trust that the answer is available through dowsing. Sometimes, it may not appear that way. On occasion, your tool might not move, or it might move strangely, or your answer may turn out not to make sense. Be sure that you have had proper training in dowsing ethics and how to ask a good question, because if you don't have that mastered, even getting in a dowsing state won't necessarily give you a meaningful answer.

Think of it this way. If you are dowsing inappropriately or using a poor question (this is common in 95% of the dowsers we see), it's tantamount to dialing a wrong number. You may use your phone well (be in a dowsing state), but if you dial the wrong number, you won't get the answer you seek. So think of dowsing as dialing the phone and getting through to the person you need to ask a question of, and having the right number is asking the right question and having proper permission. The dial tone and connection are the dowsing state.

Left Or Right Brain?

A lot of studies have been done on the functions of your left and right brain. There are some interesting tests you can see on the internet to determine which side of your brain you favor, or which side is dominant. The main point is that most people tend to approach life from either a left brain OR right brain point of view, rather than being coherent. If you understand your own dominance, you can more easily know your dowsing strengths and weaknesses and take steps to create balance.

Dowsing is an amazing, brain-balancing activity when done right, because it uses both sides of the brain. Thus, in addition to giving you answers to questions you couldn't answer rationally, it teaches you to use each side of your brain in the right and perfect way to live a better life. This sounds theoretically great, but in real life, it is a difficult goal to achieve.

Society has its own agenda and reasons for bias towards the left brain, and that overlies your natural tendency to prefer one side over the other. If you are naturally left brain dominant, you are going to be more comfortable in modern society and the educational system. If you are right brain dominant, you may constantly feel a bit out of place, denigrated or judged.

The right brain dominant viewpoint is highly creative and individual and has its strengths, as does the left brain dominant perspective. They just have opposite strengths. Artists and creative types tend to be right brain dominant, while scientists and engineers tend to be left brain dominant, although that is an oversimplification.

The truth of the matter is that we both have left and right brain abilities, and true strength comes from combining those talents, not in relying solely on half a brain to get the job done. You can't live a good life using half your brain. You can't be a masterful dowser by using only half your brain.

Thinking about your goal and forming a good dowsing question use the left brain. The actual 'dowsing' or getting the answer part uses the right brain. The dowsing state relies both sides of the brain: the left brain focuses on the dowsing question while the right brain clears the mind and opens to the answer. Perhaps this is why the dowsing state is so challenging and unique.

As a student, your left or right brain dominance will affect your ability to learn and determine your preference for certain styles of teaching. As a teacher, a person prefers an approach that speaks to her left or right brain dominance. It's taken us a long time to see these patterns and how they have impacted dowsing education and dowsing as a whole. We believe, after years of teaching dowsing a lot of different ways, that it's vital to employ a brain-balanced approach to dowsing education if we want to turn out skilled dowsers. There needs to be a logical, rational approach, but also plenty of experience and mentoring. Since dowsing is a skill, it can't be learned in one course. There need to be ways for students to refresh, upgrade and test their skill as they progress to mastery. In the past, this has not been the way dowsing education has been approached, but we have seen better results with using this method.

Although dowsing is widely regarded as an intuitive, even psychic, activity, the rational mind is an important part of the dowsing process, contrary to what many New Agers think. The New Age attracted mostly right-brain dominant individuals who had intuitive gifts and a tendency to favor them over the rational thought process. This is exactly why New Agers are thought of as fuzzy thinkers. That is also why they don't have the ability to articulate their thought processes in a logical way. They know what they know, but they can't express it clearly or in a way that is convincing to someone who has not shared their experience. This might be why shared experience is emphasized in the New Age movement, as that reduces the need to explain or articulate.

Because dowsing was characterized as a psychic talent, mostly right brain types have been attracted to it in the past. They brought with them their preconception about dowsing being a psychic activity and their bias towards using only the right brain. This led to a very incomplete approach to training people in the use of dowsing. The dowsing state and asking a good question have rarely been covered well in dowsing courses, even those given by dowsing organizations and chapters. Instead, dowsing was treated not as a skill, but a form of magic or mysticism that required no practical training. Most courses focused on getting a yes/no response with a tool and little else.

Yet taking a left brain dominant approach to dowsing is no better. Left brain types will find it easier to make a good dowsing question; they might also find it easier to focus on that question. However, they will find the dowsing state a challenge, and they will have to overcome their rational mind's desire to supply an answer, any answer, because it wants to be in charge. Too often, they merely get confirmation of what they think, instead of an actual dowsing answer. Left brain types might be more able to teach dowsing in a stepwise fashion, but their style won't always appeal to right brain dominant individuals, who prefer experiential methods, and they will find it hard to explain the intuitive aspects of dowsing

Dowsing, unlike channeling and tarot and crystal healing, attracts a lot of scientists and engineers. They are able to see that the left brain has a part in the dowsing process. Many of those scientists and engineers who are attracted to dowsing are the minority of science types who value intuition, true innovators who think in leaps and bounds, yet also understand the scientific method. An example of someone who taught dowsing from this background would be ASD (American Society of Dowsers) Past President Walt Woods. His "Letter To Robin" was a more scientific and left brain approach to dowsing than was common at the time. It may still be downloaded on the internet for free. It has obvious lacks in terms of teaching dowsing (in our opinion), but the important improvement is that it was the first widely-used lesson in America to emphasize a more logical approach in dowsing, treating it as a skill.

Right brain dominant people won't be able to describe the dowsing state beyond what it is for them (if they even describe it at all), and that often limits the ability of a student to understand and experience it. Left brain types will be tongue-tied, too, because it is so hard to describe the dowsing state even if you are articulate. So that is pretty much why the dowsing state isn't even talked about in most beginning courses.

So you can see that by becoming more aware of your own strengths and weaknesses, as determined by your preferences for left or right brain dominance, you can understand where you will need to work a bit harder to become more accurate in the dowsing process. But one big take-away is that no matter which side of your brain is dominant, you have a natural talent for some aspect of accurate dowsing.

The Concept of Allowing: A Right Brain Strength

For now, in addition to the analogy of making a phone call, listening to your Inner Voice and having silence, it is worth talking about the concept of allowing as part of the dowsing state. Allowing is hard enough to do, but the values of Western culture make it nigh on impossible. If you come from an Oriental viewpoint, you have a better chance of practicing 'allowing.' This is because Western culture emphasizes doing, while Eastern philosophy emphasizes being.

Dowsing is a combination of doing and being. To create a good dowsing question, you need to have a goal. All of those things require doing. But then you need the dowsing state to access the answer. That requires being. Being calls for a clear and empty mind, except for the dowsing question. And it also calls for allowing.

Your rational mind is not the least interested in the truth or an accurate answer or whatever you want to call it. It wants to dictate what is and is not right. It is fearful of giving power away to your intuition, because it doesn't understand or respect intuition, which is so different. You have lived most of your life using your rational mind for everything, and it has done its best, but it fails often, because as they say, if the only tool you have is a hammer, everything looks like a nail. But everything is NOT a nail.

Your left brain, at least at first, is not going to appreciate your taking away its right to make all the choices. It will throw a temper tantrum, keep your mind churning, increase your fears to shout over your Inner Voice and in general make trouble when you dowse. That is, if you are dowsing the right way. When you finally get a dowsing answer, your rational mind will tell you that you should doubt it, and so you will, because it was not obtained rationally. Dowsing is a new activity, a non-rational one that will take getting used to.

We have seen many people say they are dowsing who are not. Their rational minds are in total control. They almost always get the answer their rational mind expects. They are using dowsing to boost their confidence or justify their beliefs or attitudes, not to get answers. They aren't interested in dowsing as a way of getting answers. These people haven't heard of the dowsing state and aren't interested in it. It would cause them to become fearful if they had to dowse the right way, because they might get an answer they don't want to hear.

Allowing is generally easier for right brain dominant types. They don't have to always predict the answer. They are open to inspiration and even surprising answers. They will have problems with the left brain aspects of proper dowsing technique, like making goals and forming a question. They'll want to skip those parts and go straight to dowsing instead.

Which type are you? While you can find a test online, not all of them are very accurate. Sometimes they ask questions about your preferences, but they are preferences about things that you have probably been programmed to have certain opinions about, like whether you prefer a neat workspace. In school and at work we have all been trained to prefer a neat workspace, even if we don't care. If you are punished for daydreaming in school, you aren't likely to want to characterize yourself as a daydreamer. But remember, both types of dominance are fine, and you probably are not 100% one or the other. It will just help you to be a better dowser and more easily achieve the dowsing state if you are aware of your strengths and weaknesses.

Are you logical, analytical and rational most of the time? Do you like things laid out in linear fashion? Do you mistrust emotional decisions? Do you like math and science a lot? Are languages easy for you to learn? You may be left brain dominant.

Are you artistic, intuitive and love to dream? Do you sometimes make leaps in your thinking that don't make rational sense? Do you value emotions and innovation? Are you left-handed? You may be right brain dominant.

Overall, the dowsing state is probably going to come easier to a right brain individual than to a left brain dominant one. But anyone can learn it. And allowing the correct answer to come through is a big part of the dowsing state, one that will be blocked if your rational mind is in charge.

What You Need To Know About The Dowsing State

The dowsing state is hard to describe. It requires certain things that are easier for some people than others. Of course, that is true of any skill. If you are right brain dominant, the dowsing state part of dowsing will be easier for you. The same is true if you are an introvert or one who has practiced meditation or listening to your intuition. These will all give you a slight advantage. But in the end, anyone can learn to dowse well. Each part of the dowsing process favors a certain type or talent.

The key aspects of the dowsing state include:

- An empty, clear and peaceful mind that is detached from emotion
- Pure focus on your good dowsing question
- Allowing the answer to come through

Emptying your mind and being detached are rather challenging. Even if you have meditated, when you are dowsing, you are asking about something you are interested in. Gaining a degree of detachment can be tough. Doing so while keeping your mind clear and empty except for the question is even harder. For those who never meditated or have monkey mind, it gets even more challenging.

But that's just the first step. While you need to empty your mind to get into a dowsing state, you don't keep it empty. It's like taking all the furniture out of a room and then placing one perfect, elegant piece in the center. Now you have to keep the room empty except for that piece, which adds to the difficulty.

Adding that piece of furniture is like asking your question. And because nothing else is in the room, it's easier to focus on it. Focusing on only your dowsing question is like broadcasting the question. If it helps, think of each question having a unique frequency, and it matches the correct answer, and when you focus perfectly on it, the answer is attracted. A vague or poor question will attract an answer, but the answer will also be vague and poor. So even if you get into a dowsing state, without a good question, your answer may be useless to you.

Here's an example. You have an interest in Vitamin C for supporting your immune health and helping you avoid colds. You're in the store looking at a certain brand of Vitamin C, and you ask, "Is this Vitamin C good for me?" or "Do I need Vitamin C?" These are absolutely awful questions, but they are representative of the type of questions most dowsers ask, because they have not been taught to formulate good questions, and because in many cases, they lack the confidence or verbal talents to make it easy.

Everyone needs Vitamin C. That is the definition of a vitamin; something your body needs for good health that it cannot make itself, so it must come from your diet. And as such, Vitamin C is good for you. The answer will always be the same. So it won't be useful. When the person asked this question, instead of their dowsing state being an empty room with an exquisite piece of furniture with them focusing on the detail, they were thinking of a generic chair with no particular features.

A good dowsing question is usually long and detailed. This will make focusing on it a bit of a challenge. Saying the question over and over a number of times before getting into the dowsing state sometimes helps to lodge it in place and keeps it easier to focus on.

The last part of the process is the allowing. Remember your mind as the room you emptied, but then placed one perfect piece of furniture in the center? Think about the door to that room being open, and you're curious about what will come through it, but you aren't trying to guess. That's allowing the answer to come through. You'd think that would be easiest. You want the answer, and allowing is not doing anything. But sometimes it is the hardest part. The rational mind rarely likes the idea of you turning to another method for answers, much less if that method is intuition and some leap of faith that requires trust. Getting your rational mind to shut up and sit down during the dowsing process is a challenge if you are left brain dominant. And if you cannot succeed at it, the rational mind not only will prevent you from getting into a good dowsing state; it will supply the wrong answer, or at least the answer it thinks you want or expect. The rational mind is not content with silence or emptiness, even for a short time.

It's not always easy to tell when the rational mind is sabotaging your dowsing. Of course you can see its fingerprints when you can't calm the mind. You can usually tell if you have strong emotions, like fear of being wrong or fear of what the answer might be. And if you can't seem to lock onto your question, it could be the rational mind at work. The rational mind can slip you the answer you expect without you even suspecting it, simply by not allowing you to allow the correct answer to come through. Remember we said your tool can give an answer even if you are not in a dowsing state? Your rational mind can provide it. Last but far from least, the rational mind will tell you that you should doubt your dowsing response, because it bears no resemblance to the rational thought process.

This section gives you some good ideas as to why dowsing is a skill that takes training, time and practice to master. By now you realize that anyone who presents dowsing as just swinging a pendulum is not a real dowser. Whether they intend it or not, they are ruining the public perception of dowsing by not giving the whole story. (In most cases, they probably don't even know the whole story.)

The whole story is rich and complex, but it can also be a bit overwhelming. When you realize that even the dowsing state by itself can require hours and hours of practice to master, it can put you off dowsing, if you were hoping to master dowsing overnight. When you add the challenge of forming a good dowsing question, which requires an entire additional skill set, it becomes daunting.

But do not lose heart, dear reader! Understanding the key aspects of the dowsing state will help you to become a more accurate dowser, as it will give you the ability to improve your technique. You now know that you need to empty your mind, focus on a good question and allow the answer to come through, and that those steps are not necessarily easy, even once you understand the theory. But armed with that knowledge, you can now practice and improve your technique.

5

BRAIN WAVES & WHAT THEY SHOW

Brain Wave Basics

The dowsing state is invisible to observers. To someone watching a dowser, there is no magical trance, no sign of an altered state. The dowser picks up a pendulum or uses a deviceless method and gets a response, and the invisibility of the actual dowsing process makes it look so simple. To an observer, dowsing appears to be as straightforward as asking a question and getting an answer. Unless the dowser explains the process, an observer does not even realize that the dowsing state is the key part of dowsing...simply because you can't see it.

The simplicity of the dowsing process is part of its attraction. It also contributes to the impression that dowsing is somehow a psychic power, rather than a skill. While most masterful people make a skill look simple, whether it is playing a piano or riding a horse, the average person quickly is able to see that a great deal of skill and even talent are required for those activities. You don't sit down at a piano and play a Chopin piece unless you are skilled and trained. You don't ride a dressage horse without having a lot of practice.

It's not the same with dowsing. Anyone can pick up a pendulum and swing it. Anyone, even someone untrained, can get a 'yes' or 'no' response with a dowsing tool. Lack of proper technique is not obvious, as the most important technique is invisible: the dowsing state. As such, people can fool themselves into thinking they are dowsing when they are not, which is not the case with other skills.

It appears that many people consider themselves dowsers who never took a single course in dowsing, nor even read a book about it. They watch someone dowse; they decide it's easy; they figure anyone can do it. Sadly, those people are not really dowsing. All they have to do to confirm that fact is to dowse about things that are 'tangible target dowsing,' things that can be confirmed. Unless their answers are significantly more accurate than guessing, they are not dowsing, or at least, they aren't accurate.

Tangible target dowsing is in our opinion (and that of some of our respected colleagues) a vital part of the learning process. You get reinforcement for good technique when you get correct answers, and you get a chance to improve when you make a mistake. At least 80% of your dowsing should be this type of dowsing, not the intangible target dowsing that pervades the market. You can't learn unless you can see when you make mistakes (much like playing a piano will quickly show you how adept you are at playing a piece).

We prefer to dowse about meaningful everyday subjects rather than dowse about coin tosses and card suits. There are a number of reasons that 'tests' aren't a good training exercise for dowsing. Instead, dowse about things you need and want to know, but cannot know rationally. Our book *101 Amazing Things You Can Do With Dowsing* gives you plenty of examples, if you have difficulty thinking what to dowse about.

We believe that the reason so many people are not good at dowsing is that they aren't in a dowsing state and also lack proper training in making a good dowsing question. (We've written a book on good dowsing questions. It's an excellent companion to this book. It's much easier to describe the process of asking a good question than it is to explain the dowsing state, because the dowsing state, as we said, is invisible.)

If you watch a master dowser in action, you will see that he or she very quickly gets into a dowsing state, followed by a fairly quick answer. This is a result of a great deal of practice. You might notice that the eyes and focus of a dowser seem to shift a bit when the dowser goes into a dowsing state. It's almost like they 'check out' briefly while dowsing, then slip back to normal consciousness. It's a subtle shift, but you can sometimes see it in the eyes and body set of masterful dowsers if you know what to look for.

Unfortunately, that is about the extent of any outward sign that a dowser is in a dowsing state. The big change is going on inside the dowser, and thanks to modern science, studies are now describing the changes in brain waves that occur when dowsers dowse. This is as close as we can get to describing the dowsing state at this time. It is merely an observation of changes in the electrical activity of the brain, but it has brought us a step closer to understanding what the dowsing state is. At the very least, it has shown beyond a shadow of a doubt that there are major changes in the brain during dowsing. This is what you would expect of an altered state.

So let's talk about brain waves. There are several different types based on frequency, and each is characteristic of a particular type of activity. Most of the time, the average person is experiencing only one type of brain wave at any given time.

Different Types Of Brain Waves

It is possible to monitor brain wave patterns with various instruments. The EEG (electroencephalogram) is the best known. But there are other types, including some which give a full color pattern of the brain, showing the location and level of electrical activity at different frequencies.

For the purposes of this book, you only need to know the basics. The key brain waves are: alpha, beta, gamma, delta and theta, named after letters of the Greek alphabet. Each wave type represents a unique frequency range and typical activity pattern.

Alpha: Among the five, Alpha is at the mid-range of frequencies and is the typical waking but restful brain wave pattern, as in when you wake up in the morning, but are still lying in bed, not focusing on anything in particular. Beta and Gamma waves are higher frequencies, while Theta and Delta are lower than Alpha. When you are in an alpha state, visual input is so powerful that opening the eyes immediately adds other frequencies. (I suspect it relates more to 'focusing' the eyes than opening them, but most people who have vision will be focusing on something most of the time. I mention this, because during deviceless dowsing, we instruct dowsers to 'soft focus' or 'defocus' their eyes for best results. It may prove that this alters the brain wave state.)

Beta is the next step up in frequency from Alpha and is the 'wide awake' state, when you are focused on the outside world. Fear, anxiety and intense concentration increase this type of frequency, as does visually focusing on something.

Gamma is the next higher frequency, and it is commonly seen when learning, memory processing and idea formation are going on. This type of brain wave won't figure in the experiments on dowsers.

From these simple descriptions, you can see that Beta and Gamma brain waves are more likely to be seen when someone is focused and using their rational faculties, as in someone studying or thinking hard about a situation. The more focus and thought going on, the higher the frequency.

Theta is next lower frequency from Alpha. Theta is a state of extreme relaxation and light sleep. A person tends to be more open to hypnotic suggestion and affirmations while in this state. When added to other frequencies, it can represent access to unconscious material, inspiration or deep meditation.

Delta is the lowest frequency state, which is the wave pattern of deep, dreamless sleep. The body heals and repairs itself while in this state. When added to other frequencies, it can represent reaching out to the unknown, higher states of consciousness and the onset of paranormal phenomena.

The above descriptions are simplistic rather than exhaustive and are meant merely to give you a frame of reference to understand the complexity of brain activity and how it might relate to the dowsing state, which is a very complex altered state. While certain activities (most everyday activities) are represented by a single range of frequency, a combination are seen in a few like healing, Transcendental Meditation and dowsing.

Take A Guess

Knowing what you know about the dowsing state, what brain wave patterns would you expect to see active when a dowser is dowsing? Look at the descriptions above and think about what is involved in dowsing and the dowsing state itself. Think about the goals of dowsing and how it might work. Then speculate what brain wave(s) you would see. A bit later in this chapter, we'll discuss actual experiments that reveal the answer.

What Can Science Tell Us?

Can Science Prove Dowsing?

At this time, traditional science has little or nothing to say about dowsing. That doesn't stop people from wanting science to 'prove' dowsing. Dowsers, like anyone in a fringe group, can be a bit sensitive about being called flaky or stupid for what they believe. It's only natural to want acceptance and to wish that people would treat you with at least a modicum of respect, whether they agree with you or not. As anyone who believes in astrology or consults a psychic knows, you forfeit your right to respect if you get involved in an activity that smacks of the paranormal.

I can remember when I worked for NASA, even though I had an interest in psychic phenomena, I would make fun of people who believed in that kind of thing as if it were real. My former colleagues at NASA (at least most of them) would think I've lost my mind if they knew what I believe in now. Yet I am comfortable with it.

I accept that Science is not yet ready to confirm things like energy healing and dowsing, but that at some future time, it probably will. I know enough history of science to realize that the so-called 'truth' science promotes now will be changed over time, and anyone who lives long enough or bothers to pay attention knows this is true. I remember when butter was bad for you, and now it's not. I remember when 'better living through chemistry' was a slogan people actually liked. If you live long enough, you see things change as new facts are revealed. Science is no exception. Treating current scientific knowledge as if it is 'Truth' with a capital 'T' ignores the constantly changing nature of the body of knowledge we call Science.

One day, Science may catch up enough to describe and measure exactly what dowsing is. But I'm not going to wait for that. I can benefit from dowsing right now. Just like I don't know how exactly a TV or cell phone works, but I can use them to advantage, I am able to get great results from dowsing. I am able to put aside my ego, my need for approval and my fear of rejection, because I am so convinced of the power of dowsing.

Dr. Edith Jurka, Diplomate of the American Board of Psychiatry and Neurology, did a study on the brain waves of the dowser in 1983. She had some interesting findings that showed the dowsing state is a unique state of the brain. Her article was published in the ASD Journal, and we'll be discussing her findings in the next section of this chapter.

Just as interesting (and sadly, apparently forgotten) is her attitude about trying to 'prove' dowsing scientifically. In her article, published by the ASD, she stated:

> "If it is true that the phenomena we are trying to understand exists in a dimension without energy organized as solid matter, science as we know it now will never be able to measure it; and I feel it is futile and wasteful to try to validate any of these phenomena to the traditional scientific community."

The Problem With Science

The default skeptic's response to anything is, "That hasn't been proven scientifically." In most cases, the person who says this has no training in science or the scientific method and wouldn't know a good experimental design if it sat on him. As with most knee-jerk, unthinking and unconscious responses, this one is lame. It is lame because it implies that Science is somehow the arbiter of truth; that you need someone to tell you what you should believe. That you aren't smart enough to think for yourself, and that unless something has the scientific seal of approval, you shouldn't consider it worth looking at. All of these things are wrong.

How did Science become a religion (because that type of dogmatic approach is typical of religions)? As times changed and religions seemed to lose their grip on the minds of their followers, people turned to something else to tell them what to believe, critical thinking not being much in favor.

The really sad thing about this is that everyone is pretty much capable of rational and critical thinking if they would just take the time. An open, questioning mind learns and grows. Our educational system doesn't encourage that, because it was designed to churn out workers, not thinkers or creatives. Workers must take orders and memorize and follow faithfully whatever dogma their bosses hand down. That dictated the style of teaching and learning emphasized in schools and universities. What we have is a society of un-conscious people who don't really want to think. They want to be told what to think.

Real scientists--and they are in the minority--are not dogmatic. They are inventive, intuitive and quest for knowledge. The best scientists have theories they want to test, but they are not too attached to them, because that would lead them astray as they seek accurate answers. Real scientists, like real dowsers, need to be open to hearing whatever the answer is, regardless of how incredible or unwanted.

We respect real scientists, but we do not confuse them with conventional, dogmatic prigs who populate Science and have turned it into a religion. Real scientists understand that change is part of science. What was regarded as scientific truth hundreds of years ago (the sun revolves around the earth; the earth is flat) is now acknowledged to be laughably false. Just as the belief of a couple hundred years ago that bleeding a person would aid in healing, or that it wasn't important to wash when handling patients with infections is now conveniently forgotten to have been scientific Truth at that time. Those formerly 'scientific' beliefs are now considered horrifically stupid, but in their time, those who argued against them were vilified (considered backward and ignorant), much the same way that people now laugh at dowsers. It's not so bad being in the company of innovators and geniuses like Galileo and Semmelweis, is it?

It is discouraging that modern scientists by and large seem unable to extrapolate from history. Germ theory and the proper ordering of the solar system were accepted only after instruments supported the new theories. It didn't matter that there was plenty of proof in other ways to cause a re-examination of the system. They weren't interested. One can easily imagine someone in Galileo's time saying, "That hasn't been scientifically proven to be true" when discussing whether the earth revolved around the sun or vice versa. Copernicus was so frightened of the Church's reaction (at that time, the Church, not Science, was whom everyone looked to) that he deliberately held off publishing his carefully researched treatise.

This same attitude is the hallmark of people who denigrate dowsing and energy work simply because science lags behind in making instruments to show what is happening. They lack the imagination and the critical thinking skills to evaluate dowser's claims, and they downright ignore plenty of proof that dowsing works. But this is the pattern in humanity when faced with changing their beloved beliefs. It isn't just a campaign against dowsing.

What Is The Appropriate Response?

The reaction many dowsers have to dogmatic and negative treatment from conventional people is to try to gain their approval by finding a way to make dowsing appear scientific. But is accepting Science as the new arbiter of Truth going to ultimately solve the problem of the credibility of dowsing? No. If Science is not capable of making an accurate judgment about dowsing at this time, it isn't wise to give it the power to say whether dowsing is real.

If you study history, you will be able to predict that only when science finally catches up--and make no mistake, that is what it is doing, playing catch up--and finds a way to have an instrument show what is going on when a dowser dowses, only then will Science endorse dowsing. Then, seeing that confirmation on their twinkly-lights, they will believe in dowsing. And once they accept it, they will forget their previous obnoxious behavior. (Consider acupuncture, for example, and the winding journey it took from when it was first brought to Western medicine. In the beginning, medicine poked fun at acupuncture. Much later, it took over and tried to make it impossible for anyone but a doctor to practice it. A complete turnaround, including an unwillingness to even admit to the former negative attitude. Typical of the evolution of Science.)

Science cannot verify to its satisfaction that dowsing works. We would be wise to learn from history and find other means to make our case. Using words like 'quantum' and 'entanglement' incorrectly, hoping that scientific terms will lend authority to dowsing, only makes things worse. New Agers are too willing to throw around terms they cannot even explain, hoping to gain credibility. Dowsers would be wise to avoid that pattern.

Being willing to wait for science to catch up is the best strategy. Don't agree that science must prove dowsing. Don't accept their terms. Science cannot at this time prove much of anything about dowsing. Nor can it disprove dowsing. Let science grow and stop being afraid of the disrespect and criticism of people who are unthinking and prejudiced. Become an accurate dowser and laugh as you improve your life measurably. You don't need the blessing of Science.

Is There Any Appropriate Scientific Angle?

Yes, there is usefulness in a scientific approach, but most people are not qualified to examine dowsing scientifically. If you are not a trained experimental scientist, you can end up doing more harm than good by 'practicing' science. It's like someone trying to do brain surgery who never went to medical school. Science is a skill that requires education and training.

There are some good scientists working to expand our knowledge and the credibility of dowsing and various other metaphysical subjects. Science is not a hobby and should not be practiced by those who are untrained in it. Support real scientists and take the time to read and question experimental studies and learn to think critically about them.

In the next section we'll be looking at actual experiments on the dowsing state. We will comment on their contribution and what they leave unanswered, as well as some problems with the experimental design and conclusions that would make 'real' scientists reluctant to accept the results.

. . .

The Scientific Proof

Scientific proof of dowsing (in the form of laboratory experiments that give hard data about what goes on during the dowsing process) is sorely lacking in the U.S. It is possible that in Russia, where 'psychic' phenomena lack the stigma they carry in the West, there have been more scientific studies on the dowsing process, but they are not readily available.

The only two scientific studies of the dowsing state that we could find were both published in the journal of the American Society of Dowsers, one in 1983, and the other in two parts, one in 1997, the other in 1998. These studies were done using different instruments, and both yielded remarkably similar results, showing that the dowsing state does appear to be an altered brain state characterized by a unique set of brain waves showing remarkable coherence.

In spite of the exciting results, it is necessary to point out that there are some deficiencies in the studies that would cause traditional science to question the results. These are commented on in some detail below. Regardless, the studies shed light on the dowsing state. It would be fascinating to do extensive studies on a large number of accurate dowsers and see whether these conclusions hold up. We expect they would, and only play devil's advocate so future studies may be even better designed and well-received.

The Work Of Dr. Edith Jurka in 1983

To the best of our knowledge, this was the first attempt in the U.S. at a scientific study of the dowsing process, and it focused on measuring the brain activity of dowsers while dowsing.

Summary Of Results

The Mind Mirror was the instrument used in this study. It consists of two EEGs hooked together such that they give you a picture of both hemispheres of the brain. The image drawn by the instrument shows bilaterally symmetrical pictures of brain activity, where brain waves of each frequency make a sort of outward 'blip' on the drawing. As expected, a blip showed up in the delta range for deeply sleeping subject, while those who were falling asleep registered theta waves. Restful but awake subjects had a bulge in alpha waves, and wide awake people had a large blip in beta. But only one type of wave at any time was observed in 'normal' people doing 'normal' things.

Practitioners of Transcendental Meditation (TM) showed a large alpha bulge plus a smaller theta blip while meditating. Zen meditation and lucid awareness yielded beta, alpha and theta blips. Dowsers had a unique pattern, showing beta, alpha, theta and delta bulges on the Mind Mirror. Ed Stillman in his later study pointed out that sometimes muscle movements can cause an artifact in delta waves on both the Mind Mirror and the Lexicon machines (the types of EEGs used in these studies), so that the delta wave results should be taken as less reliable than the other frequencies observed when extrapolated from dowsers using tools, because it was possible that their muscle movements led to spurious delta measurements. Regardless, the dowsers clearly showed vastly different brain waves from other subjects, and in Stillman's studies, which used another instrument, the delta phenomenon was repeated. More significantly, it was repeated in subjects who were not using tools to dowse.

Dr. Cade, who pioneered research using the Mind Mirror, tested over 3000 subjects. He particularly studied yogis and healers and described what he called the 5th level of states of consciousness, which was characterized by wide alpha, moderate beta and theta and no delta waves. Measured in psychic healers while healing, the 5th state, when held stable, induced a similar state in the healee, who otherwise did not exhibit the 5th state at all. During the healing process, the amplitude of the 5th state in the healer decreased, while it grew in the healee.

This 5th state was present in dowsers, in addition to a delta state, which Dr. Jurka concluded indicated the 'searching' part of the process of dowsing. The brain wave patterns of dowsers when dowsing are similar to those of yogis and psychic healers. Because this paper was not in a scientific journal, further speculation was added to the conclusions as to what is going on in the brain of a dowser when dowsing, and how this 5th state relates to dowsing. The conclusions are attractive to any dowser and stimulate a lot of questions about the dowsing process that are unanswered to this day.

The Work Of Ed Stillman in 1997

The best study on the dowsing state was published in 1997-98 in "The American Dowser," the quarterly digest of the American Society of Dowsers. See the Resources section for the citation. This study was a big step forward in revealing that the dowsing state really exists and is different from any other type of brain state. New instruments and methodology in the 97-98 study yielded some very interesting and convincing results while supporting Jurka's results. The authors are to be congratulated for helping to move dowsing forward in terms of the understanding of the dowsing state.

Summary Of Results

The Lexicor Neurosearch is an advanced (as of 1997) EEG machine that yields color images of the brain that show not only the brain wave frequencies, but activity levels of any brain waves on both sides of the brain. It measures activity in a totally different way from the equipment used in Dr. Jurka's work in 1983, which lends further credence to the results, since Ed Stillman's results support and add to what Dr. Jurka found.

Subjects were tested while dowsing with a tool and while dowsing devicelessly with eyes closed. In both cases, a combination of alpha, theta, beta and delta brain waves were recorded during the dowsing process, with even more coherence during the deviceless dowsing. It was noted that delta brain waves may not be accurately measured using this technique, so plans were made to measure delta wave activity differently at a future date. However, it does not appear that study ever took place.

The results also indicate that 7 of the 8 dowsers tested entered a different altered brain state when dowsing devicelessly, as opposed to the altered state while using a tool. This altered state was indicative of the limbic brain (or brain stem, the non-intellectual part of the brain) giving information to the cerebral cortex, the intellectual part. Results were consistent when taken 10 months apart on the same subject. It is particularly convincing that using a different instrument, Ed Stillman repeated Dr. Jurka's earlier results.

Ed summarizes (italics are his):

> "The states are characterized by simultaneous *coherent delta*; now known to be produced in other meditative states in addition to without the subject being asleep, *coherent theta*; including contact with the subconscious mind, the visual component of imagery, and loss of time sense; *coherent alpha*; with the deep pillow of silence, quiet, beautiful both-hemisphere coherence; and *coherent beta*; with creative cognition, thought and intellectual analysis during the asking of dowsing questions and receiving the answers."

What is Coherence?

Coherence is a term you see frequently when you read about brain waves. So it's important you have an idea what this means before we go further. From the Ed Stillman study:

> "The term "coherence" provides a measure of the correlation between two EEG records for a given frequency range and from different areas of the brain. If large quantities of the neurons in the spatially separated brain areas are firing simultaneously, and are firing in phase with each other (firing at the same time), there will be a large increase in the absolute brain power levels. The increase could be in the theta, alpha or beta bands or, as we found in the dowsers tested, high coherence levels in all of these bands at the same time."

So, high coherence is positive, and dowsers were seen to have coherence across frequencies rather than in just one (as in normal activities) or two (as in meditation). It was fascinating that deviceless dowsing with eyes shut yielded coherence in all waves, including Beta, which is normally active only when eyes are open and focused. The high level of Beta wave coherence when the dowsers dowsed with no tool and eyes closed indicates thoughts and visions coming directly to the cortex from the limbic brain system (the brain stem). To have high beta with eyes closed implies an altered state of consciousness. The Stillman study explains:

> "Walt had entered a state where limbic brain (brain stem) "pictures" and subconscious images were providing information directly to the cerebral cortex. Stated differently, "in deviceless dowsing, Walt had entered an altered state of consciousness where non-intellect is dominating consciousness and giving information directly to the cerebral cortex. It is as if Walt had projected the limbic brain system (the brain stem) into the earth to receive his water dowsing data."

Experimental Design Issues

The Stillman study had planned to test 14, but in the end, only subjected 8 'gifted' dowsers to testing. This is not a large enough sample size to draw sweeping conclusions. Ideally, you would want to see test results from a large number of masterful dowsers.

There is no clear definition (meaning scientifically reproducible) of what 'gifted' meant, nor any sign that these dowsers passed any kind of test, nor what criteria were used to label them as 'gifted'. Walt Woods, then president of the ASD, was one of the subjects, and of course it would be accepted that he was masterful, yet for scientific purposes, acclamation is not adequate. We expect that Dr. Jurka also chose her subjects based on a consensus of opinions, but that is not totally reliable in terms of choosing people who are truly talented at a skill. This might explain the variation she saw in the results.

Subjects in addition to not having to meet any criteria to be judged good at dowsing were (except in one case) anonymous, so there is no way to judge how good they were years after the study was completed. It's necessary to accept that the opinion of Ed Stillman as to who is good at dowsing is something every dowser would agree with. While we have every respect for Ed and his judgment, that is not really a scientific way to choose subjects.

The ASD journal has no stature scientifically because it accepts just about any article; it has no scientific peer review, so it is not subject to the 'rigorous' process that supposedly separates the wheat from the chaff. Often, in the bigger journals, peer review has too much to do with what's popular and what's not, but there is merit in having other members of a field (who have stature) comment on the work and make sure it meets certain criteria in terms of design before it is published, as in the scientific world, publication yields a degree of acceptance.

Another issue in addition to small sample size is that too many variables changed; the trials went from pendulum dowsing to deviceless, but also had the subjects close their eyes when using no tool. This violates good procedure, as only one variable should be changed at a time, or your conclusions can't really be justified. Having them keep eyes open and soft focus might have been better. They switched to deviceless dowsing with eyes shut and then decided that shutting the eyes was the key to the change, when it was really only one aspect of the change in technique. Perhaps the deviceless method caused the observed change, and it had nothing to do with whether eyes were shut or not. (It is our suspicion that not having a tool to focus on improves the coherence of the brain waves and the connection with the subconscious.) This technique is also bothersome in that deviceless dowsing is not always practiced with the eyes shut, so any conclusions made would not necessarily apply to all deviceless dowsing.

In spite of what a conventional scientist might call flaws in the design, the findings of the study are quite compelling, and to anyone who believes in dowsing, they are fascinating. This study showed that the brain wave patterns of dowsers when in the dowsing state are uniquely different from a normal waking state, and we believe that conclusion to be true, even if the results of the experiment would not be acceptable to conventional science.

6

AN ALTERED STATE OF CONSCIOUSNESS?

Is The Dowsing State Always The Same?

The preliminary results of the Jurka and Stillman studies indicate that there is definitely a difference in brain wave patterns during dowsing. Although we'd love to see a broader study with many more subjects and clearer qualifications for being considered a masterful dowser, the important conclusion is that dowsing, done properly, changes your brain wave patterns.

The patterns of masterful dowsers, as noted by Ed Stillman, are similar but not identical to those of healers and those who practice Transcendental Meditation (TM). Stillman also quoted a study by Dr. Maxwell Cade that showed that delta waves are only noted in waking conditions "during higher levels of consciousness, at the onset of paranormal phenomena, or when reaching out to the unknown." The latter reference is not explained in Stillman's article (though it is a clear analogy to dowsing), but the first two, higher levels of consciousness and paranormal phenomena, will not surprise dowsers, since dowsing has long been listed as a psychic ability. For those of us who don't like characterizing it as such, the "higher levels of consciousness" rings a bell. We believe dowsing is a natural human skill that anyone can master, but as a skill, it requires practice and proper technique to reach this higher level of consciousness. In our book, *Dowsing: Practical Enlightenment*, we make a strong case for dowsing as a way to raise one's level of consciousness and live a more enlightened lifestyle, but that result only comes through mastery of dowsing. Just dowsing now and then does not yield the results.

But even when 'mastered'--that term is yet to be defined clearly--does the dowsing state always look alike in terms of brain wave patterns? The answer Ed Stillman got was 'no.' There were consistent differences between dowsers who used tools, eyes opened, and subjects who dowsed devicelessly, eyes shut. As noted in the previous chapter, it's a shame that Stillman changed two variables during the test--eyes open/shut; use of tool/no tool--as that means it's impossible to say for sure which variable was responsible for the difference in results.

He speculated that maybe all dowsers should not look at their tools, should close their eyes while dowsing, as the brain wave patterns of the deviceless dowsers was coherent across a broader frequency than those using a tool. For many years, we have advocated teaching dowsers deviceless dowsing first and foremost, because it is our belief that starting with a tool has many detrimental side effects, diminishing effectiveness. We can now add this observation to those. We dowse almost exclusively without tools, and we believe it is the more natural and accurate way to dowse.

A tool is very helpful in certain situations, and we are not saying tools should never be employed, just that one should use deviceless dowsing unless there is a compelling reason to use a tool. A masterful dowser can no doubt get accurate answers with a tool, eyes wide open. But it now appears that the dowsing state of that dowser is measurably different from that of a dowser dowsing without tools, eyes shut, and the broader coherence across frequencies obtained by the deviceless dowser should encourage you to put your tool aside and master deviceless dowsing.

Our interpretation for the observed differences in brain waves is that it's the lack of tool that matters. We encourage students to soft focus when dowsing devicelessly, which means not looking at anything. That, in our opinion, should give similar results to closing the eyes. The visual focus on the tool diminishes the brain coherence during the dowsing state, which is restored if one dowses devicelessly, no focus on external objects, but looking within.

Increasing theta and delta waves has been shown to enhance intuition. This may explain a perception that dowsers have as they master dowsing. Often, they find that their intuition in general improves. They are able to get 'gut feelings' more easily. By learning to dowse well, being able to get in a dowsing state and practicing dowsing often, you will increase your delta and theta frequencies in the brain and most probably, notice improvement in your intuitive abilities.

Most research suggests that if you can become consciously aware in the delta brainwave state, you will have a nearly perfect sense of intuition

This may explain why we have found that as we became accomplished dowsers, we often did not have to dowse about something in order to know the answer. If you're interested in learning more about different brain waves and what they mean, we recommend you read *Understanding Your Brain Waves* by Dr. Jeffrey Fannin. The white paper may be obtained for free on the internet.

Is the Dowsing State Only For Dowsing?

Scientific research shows that it is very unusual to have coherent brain waves in multiple frequencies simultaneously, but dowsing is not the only instance of this. Psychic healers exhibit this pattern, and it appears they entrain the healee to adopt that coherence, and that may be what brings on healing. This state is also noted at the onset of paranormal activity. (Healing of the type we refer to might be considered by some to be miraculous or paranormal.) Brain wave patterns similar to the dowsing state have also been observed in 'higher levels of consciousness,' though it might be hard to agree on exactly what that means. As referenced in Ed Stillman's studies, some gurus who exhibit strange powers, for example, show this type of brain wave coherence.

Meditation does not include delta or beta frequencies, and thus meditation in general is not going to produce a state equivalent to the dowsing state. However, Dr. Joe Dispenza's work on the placebo effect may be training people to have a dowsing state-like brain wave pattern. He has shown that you can harness the body's ability to heal by entering a certain state that he describes as making you the placebo. His technique involves meditation, which we know stimulates coherence in alpha and theta frequencies simultaneously, plus focusing on changing limiting beliefs and having a health goal, which, much like dowsing, gives a focus and creates a searching pattern, adding activity in delta and beta. The EEGs of his subjects do show in many cases activity in all four types of brain waves that would argue something much like the dowsing state is going on. His technique is used for self-healing and it is easy to see how it could also be used to improve conscious manifestation of your other life goals.

What does this mean for you, both in dowsing and in the rest of your life? If you set out to master dowsing and use it a lot, you will train your brain to have coherence across the four types of brain waves we've been talking about. This will enhance your intuition overall as well as improve your dowsing accuracy. But it has other spinoffs. If you are interested in a healing technique, the mastery of the dowsing state may well help you to become a more effective healer. If you are interested in improving your own health, the dowsing state (as shown by Dr. Dispenza) is crucial for that. If you are seeking spiritual enlightenment, you will be following in the footsteps of many seekers, and your spiritual connection may be enhanced by virtue of your facility at reaching the dowsing state. Your ability to manifest the outcomes you desire may well be accelerated by your mastery of the dowsing state. You might even develop abilities that are called 'psychic.'

In fact, we probably should have a special name for this state other than the dowsing state. It appears that it is critical in many activities that are of interest to spiritual seekers and healers. Dowsing hasn't yet captured the interest of very many people. But the dowsing state is the gateway to incredible powers and a greatly improved life, and we're pretty sure that's something most people are interested in.

Living in the Dowsing State

When we started researching for this book, we also intuitively felt it would be useful to live the dowsing state, instead of saving it just for dowsing. After researching the topic, we're convinced there are amazing benefits to mastering the dowsing state and using it as part of your everyday life. As Ed Stillman concluded:

> "Once these globally expanded dowsing brainwave patterns are learned by repeated dowsing, they are constantly reinforced as dowsing prowess and progress increases and improves. The dowsing brainwave patterns become a part of the dowser's daily life. The dowser has a multifaceted emerging interaction and a natural culture emerges."

Most adult humans spend the majority of their waking time in the Beta state. This state has a number of advantages, but it also has disadvantages. Anxiety, stress, a lack of connection to Spirit are side effects of living dominantly in Beta. By adding in the other brainwaves, you have coherence and harmony in your life. There is less stress, a greater connection to Spirit, a strong intuition, a feeling of calm.

Each state has its up and down sides, but by living in all the states in a balanced way, you achieve a higher level of consciousness and harmony by far than the average person. You may not become a yogi, but you can experience some of the blessings they experience.

Modern culture emphasizes Beta activities to the exclusion of others. Native peoples have a much closer connection to Nature and a sense of being in the present moment that eludes most humans. It is likely their brain waves would be significantly different. Beyond that, the coherent brain wave state seen during dowsing is a conscious, aware and engaged state that would seem to be just what one needs to do magic and make miracles happen.

It may be that after you have totally mastered the dowsing state and dowsing, you would be so in touch with your intuition that you wouldn't even need to dowse to know what is best for you. You might be able to easily manifest the outcomes you desire. Indeed, you could possibly heal yourself and others with ease.

Perhaps this is one reason that some people promote dowsing more as magic than as an intuitive skill. The dowsing state is apparently a magical one of great power for improving your life in many ways. The problem with those who try to sell dowsing as simply spinning a pendulum and wishing for outcomes is that they have skipped the critical part of the process--the mastery of the dowsing state and all that goes along with that altered state. Surveys we have taken of large numbers of dowsers show that most people are unfamiliar with how to get into the dowsing state. Most will find it challenging at first and require plenty of practice to master it.

Some dowsing 'gurus' prefer not to address this fact, and they make dowsing look like magic. Well, dowsing might lead you to have miraculous outcomes and changes in your life, but only if you master it. Swinging a pendulum is not dowsing mastery. Asking questions is not dowsing mastery. The dowsing state is the core of accurate dowsing, and it takes time and practice to master it. But once done, you might expand your skill to include intuition in general, healing, paranormal phenomena and manifesting mastery.

7

HOW TO GET INTO A DOWSING STATE?

So How Do You Do It?

It's all very well to say how valuable mastery of the dowsing state is and exhort you to use it in your everyday life, but how do you get into the dowsing state? How do you know you're in it? How do you master it?

Sadly, most courses don't spend a great deal of time on this subject, because it's pretty tricky to teach. If you had the EEG machine Ed Stillman was using, you could tell if someone was in a dowsing state or not. But they're hard to come by. So most courses give you a brief description and let you try to sort it out. And that is a huge mistake, because it's a challenging topic.

As you know from reading this book, the dowsing state is different from your normal waking state. That's why they call it an altered state. To get answers to questions your rational mind cannot provide you with requires that you reach out into the unknown, deep into your subconscious or the unconscious to get the answers. That cannot be done in a normal waking state.

Because of the difficulty of teaching this part of the dowsing process, it turns out that many dowsers are not actually dowsing. They can ask a question, get calm and spin their tool, and they get an answer, but they aren't dowsing, because they're not in the dowsing state. We need to remind you again: the dowsing state is not optional.

As a reminder, here are the key aspects of the dowsing state:

- An empty, clear and peaceful mind that is detached from emotion
- Pure focus on your good dowsing question and nothing else
- Sending the question out and allowing the answer to come through

It's not easy to break the dowsing state into steps, but this is one way of looking at it. Then, you will need to address each aspect and put them together. We're going to take it step by step and give you some suggestions for success.

Please note that there is no one set of steps or rituals guaranteed to get you into a dowsing state. Much depends on you as an individual. Anyone who promises you can reach a dowsing state by doing this or saying that is mistaken. You must feel your way into the dowsing state and learn the sign of when you have achieved it and how different it feels from a regular waking state, and no one can tell you exactly how to do that. We can only describe various methods and make suggestions that we believe will help you learn to recognize and reproduce it.

How Do You Clear Your Mind?

Meditation is hands down the easiest way to learn to clear your mind. If you have monkey mind, guided visualizations are a good first step. They give your mind one thing to do while you learn to stop multi-tasking.

Success will come quicker if you learn to do this throughout your daily life. That means stop multi-tasking. Do one thing at a time. This will help you reduce monkey mind.

Learn to stay in the present moment. Spend less time dwelling in the past or worrying about the future. Monitor your thoughts and particularly your words. Don't allow yourself to get caught up in past drama and retell the story to everyone you meet. That traps you in the past. Learn to let go of fear and worries--we've found EFT, the Emotional Freedom Technique--to be very helpful with that. We've used it for years with good results. Some people like The Emotion Code for releasing emotions. Find something that works for you. You can't fool yourself about detachment. You'll know what works.

Mastering dowsing and the dowsing state is easier if you begin to approach all of your daily life the way you do your dowsing. It will take time to build new neural pathways, but you will be pleased with the results.

How Can You Detach From Emotions?

Emotions are your guidance system in life. It isn't wise to judge or suppress them. So we aren't suggesting you do that. It's vital to face your emotions. If you have emotions you consider negative, it's a warning that you are straying from the path that will bring you the most happiness. Deal with whatever is causing the fear or anger. Don't suppress negative emotions.

Once you learn to stay more in present moment, as described above, you will notice you spend less time worrying, anxious or fearful. Those emotions are often signs you are not in present moment. Having a self-help technique like the tapping therapy is a must for seeing progress.

It is natural to have fears and worries, but you want to minimize them and remove them from the dowsing process. If you are asking a dowsing question that you absolutely cannot detach from, you shouldn't try to dowse. Advanced dowsing, like in life and death situations, should only be done by those who have mastered proper dowsing technique. Start with less stressful subjects to master basic dowsing technique, then move on to topics that trigger concerns and practice setting aside your emotions.

To dowse accurately, you need to have a curious attitude. You want the answer, whatever it is, and you are willing to accept whatever it is, because having the answer is better than not having the answer. When you have the answer, you are a step ahead and can take right action. It is surprising how many people really don't want to know the truth if it's something they think is 'bad,' but even knowing something 'bad' gives you a better chance of a positive outcome than not knowing. Most people have to learn how to accept bad news. It isn't easy, and you shouldn't feel upset that it takes time and practice. You will notice a positive halo effect in your everyday life once you master this, because you will learn that knowing the answers is a good thing, and that fear does not help you live a better life.

How Do You Stay Focused On Your Dowsing Question?

When you're just starting, you might find it useful to do self-hypnosis to practice focusing. Self-hypnosis really works, and it's inexpensive to do. The guided visualization will help you focus on the process and shut out the outside world. And you might get some great results. Then, when you go to dowse, you will be familiar with how you want to feel during the dowsing process. Please note we're not saying dowsing is about self-hypnosis; we're just saying that if you practice self-hypnosis for personal growth, it will help you learn to recognize and get into a dowsing state when you dowse, because the brain state during self-hypnosis is similar to that of dowsing, in that it takes more than one type of brain wave.

We've said that a dowsing question is usually long and detailed. It is wise to write your question down and refine it carefully. Then say the question out loud several times and get a 'feel' for it. Let it sink into your consciousness. Block out anything else but the question. Say it over and over until you feel truly focused on it in a relaxed and curious way. Don't feel silly doing this. Even now, when we dowse, we usually say a long question multiple times before actually dowsing it. It's like taking the time to tune a radio to your favorite station. Once you feel dialed in, it's time to dowse.

How Do You Allow The Answer To Come Through?

If you've made it this far with success, this step is pretty easy. Your rational mind might try to hijack the process at this point, attempting to insert the answer it expects. Hopefully you have spent time telling your rational mind to sit down and shut up when you are dowsing. The meditation and self-hypnosis practice will help with this, but in the silence after you ask the dowsing question, you need to be comfortable waiting for the answer to come. Usually, it comes pretty quickly. But newbies sometimes find that it takes longer than they wish. If you're new, be patient and know that it will speed up over time. But you cannot artificially force it to go faster. You have to curb your impatience and the doubt your rational mind throws your way like dust in your face. Like all the other aspects of the dowsing state, this one takes time for most people to master. Just be patient with yourself.

How Can You Tell?

So you've practiced and practiced, and you're still doubting whether you are in a dowsing state when you dowse. That's OK. It's natural. It takes time to learn to sense something this subtle. We are so used to focusing outward and using our physical senses to interpret big sensory cues that we tend to ignore subtle inner ones.

Learning to be still and silent will help you notice. Practice being an observer of your own body and sensations. When you dowse, do you feel calm, or do you feel fearful about what the answer will be? Negative emotions or strong emotions of any kind are a sign that you aren't in the dowsing state.

Feeling calm and still, but wondering if you are actually in the dowsing state? That's normal at first, too. Everyone goes through that stage. It's easier to tell when you are NOT in the dowsing state than when you are, at least at first. Strong emotions, monkey mind and a lack of focus on the question are all signs you are not in a dowsing state. Don't dowse when you feel that way.

But when you are calm, clear and focused and have a curious attitude and an open mind about the answer, you may still wonder when the answer comes if you were actually in the dowsing state. Set that worry aside. Look at the answer. How did it feel when you got the answer? Did it feel like it came out of nowhere, or did it feel like part of your rational thought process? That seems a strange question, but for me at least, I feel answers are injected into me when I am dowsing, but when I am thinking, the answers my brain provides are from a logical sequence of thoughts. I am able to feel the difference. It's almost like the answers come from another place when dowsing. We've talked about the possible sources of dowsing answers, and we can't prove where they come from, but we do know they don't come from the rational mind, so when they come, it won't feel quite the same as a rational thought process. This is a subtle distinction, but you will eventually learn to spot it.

Another reinforcing experience is when you get an answer that surprises you. When you get an unexpected answer, you can be sure your rational mind didn't provide it. Unexpected answers are usually correct, although you should follow good dowsing procedure and make sure your polarity isn't flipped, etc. But when you know you've followed proper technique and the answer shocks you, it's almost always correct. People who never get surprised when dowsing are probably not dowsing.

As you master dowsing, you will find that the answers often arrive almost before you finish asking the question. This is a sign of mastery and progress. Ideally, your goal of mastering dowsing should be that you can easily get accurate answers quickly when you focus on a question. This is another reason to abandon tool use. Tools slow the process and are usually just a crutch for accentuating the yes/no answer. Using your body directly to dowse will more quickly train you to the dowsing response. You will learn to read your body instead of focusing on the tool. As the studies of brain waves suggest, you can ultimately become amazingly intuitive if you master the dowsing state.

Granted, all of the above are rather subtle, but part of mastering dowsing is learning to tune in to your Inner Voice, which is very quiet. And learning to read your body and the signs it gives you are part of the mastery process.

Each person is unique, so we can't give you a universal list of cues and signals. But you will eventually learn when your body is trying to tell you that you aren't able to dowse or get in a dowsing state. Some possible signs of not being in a dowsing state include:

- An inability to focus on the question, no matter how hard you try
- Strange reactions with your tool, if you are using one
- A feeling of things 'not being right' as you try to dowse
- A particular physical symptom, like an eye twitch or ache somewhere
- A picture of something that comes to mind whenever you are unable to dowse (more common in visual people)
- When using a scale, you might get a certain number to indicate something is 'off' in the dowsing process; for Maggie, it's the number 3. When you get that number, ask if it represents the actual number or something else.

- Sometimes when you get the answer you expect, and you get it really fast, you may not be in a dowsing state (although you need to learn how to distinguish this from an accurate answer that comes to a veteran dowser)
- If you are feeling any negative emotions like fear, you are not in a dowsing state

The above are all things you will have to observe and associate with whatever the message is. If you dowse enough, patterns will emerge. If you don't dowse often, the rare subtle cues will escape you. So be sure to dowse often and notice patterns that might be trying to tell you that you can't dowse accurately or aren't able to get in a dowsing state.

There are always going to be subjects you cannot dowse about, either for ethical reasons or because it is just inappropriate, though you may not know why. Being able to tell if your dowsing is off is vital.

What About Accuracy?

How can you tell your dowsing answers are accurate? Do you assume that if you get into a dowsing state, the answers are correct? No. The dowsing state is the core of good dowsing, but it isn't the only requirement for accuracy, alas. As with any skill, there are key aspects to dowsing that can disrupt the process or give you an invalid response.

If you have a bad question, you will get a bad answer, even if you are in the dowsing state. This book is not about making good questions, but that topic is vital to success. We recommend our book *Ask The Right Question: The Essential Sourcebook Of Good Dowsing Questions* for that topic.

Once you master the dowsing state and forming good questions, does that guarantee your answers are correct? Don't we wish! There are other factors that contribute to wrong answers. Flipped polarity is a common one. We cover this topic in our dowsing courses. Your body has a natural polarity, and if it flips, 'yes' becomes 'no' and vice versa. There are many contributing factors to reversed polarity, and you need to learn how to recognize and correct it. We recommend our courses if you haven't taken them.

Assuming you have mastered and checked all of the above, you still need to be aware that dowsing is not 100%. Nothing in life is. Your rational mind doesn't always come to accurate conclusions or decisions in spite of years of training, and you accept that. Learn to accept that dowsing isn't always going to be accurate. When your answers are incorrect, it will almost always trace back to some problem with polarity, your question or not being in a dowsing state for some reason. Even the most advanced dowsers can get wrong answers. We'll talk later about learning when not to dowse. That will improve your record and accuracy.

How can you come to trust your dowsing answers? Earlier we urged you to do tangible target dowsing at least 80% of the time you dowse. We explained that tangible target dowsing isn't about card suits and coin tosses, although those are tangible. We believe dowsing is best used in a natural way. Dowsing is to help you make choices, to get information you need or want to have. Get our book *101 Amazing Things You Can Do With Dowsing* and start dowsing every day. Start with simple things your brain can't help you with. Our book gives you plenty of examples, gives you good questions and tells you how to interpret answers.

When you start dowsing regularly to pick a book or movie, to select an item on a restaurant menu and to pick a gift for a family member, you will get feedback that proves whether you were correct or not in many cases. That will help you build confidence. Then you can move on to more challenging subjects for dowsing. Don't rush to health dowsing or big subjects until you are confident.

While no one is 100% accurate, a masterful dowser will often be 90%+ accurate in their specialty. Remember that there are many topics you can dowse about. Water dowsers will generally be 95%+ accurate if they are masterful. But can a water dowser expect 95% accuracy when dowsing about health? No. You need to recognize your limitations in terms of experience. Each specialty in dowsing has its own vocabulary, pitfalls and learning curve. Don't let that discourage you. Just use it to be realistic about your expectations for accuracy. If you dowse enough about a topic, and you have the intention of mastering it, you will succeed.

Can't Always Get In Dowsing State?

This section is for those who do know how to get into a dowsing state and can tell for sure when they are not. If you have mastered the basics of dowsing and the dowsing state, but you sometimes find you cannot reach it, there are reasons. Don't be hard on yourself for not being consistently able to access the dowsing state. There is a reason this is happening, and it's an opportunity for you to take your dowsing to the next level.

If you sometimes feel you are able to get into a dowsing state, and sometimes not, look for patterns. What are you dowsing about those times you can't get into a dowsing state? Does it predominately happen when you are health dowsing? Dowsing about yourself? Dowsing about money?

Some topics are going to be harder for you to dowse about than others. When you dowse about health, you may be worried. You will notice that you have emotions and concerns. You need to deal with those concerns before you dowse. There are also probably beliefs behind those emotions. This isn't a book about clearing beliefs, but the ability to clear beliefs is a very helpful skill to have when you want to shift your outlook. Or you can use a tapping therapy. We use both often.

What if you can't see a pattern in the topics themselves? Perhaps it just happens when you are dowsing about things you have attachment to. Most of us have issues with money and health. If you can dowse about things that aren't life or death, but you have trouble getting into a dowsing state for big topics, don't beat yourself up. Becoming an advanced dowser requires you to change your outlook on life. You need to get a grip on your emotions, stay in present time and let go of attachments and judgments. There are no short cuts to that. You need to employ whatever tools or therapies will help you achieve those things. There is no one-size-fits-all way.

What if there is no pattern in terms of dowsing topic or your emotions? Perhaps you will discover you need to dowse earlier in the day. You don't dowse well when you are tired. Or maybe you notice you have inaccuracies when you dowse in a certain location. Check for environmental energies that might be reversing your polarity and fix them. If you're new to dowsing, find a peaceful place to dowse. Don't dowse in a busy location with lots of distractions. Be sure you are fully hydrated. Polarity shifts are common when you are dehydrated.

Don't be hard on yourself. Learning a skill is a journey. As you master dowsing and the dowsing state, you will see so many spinoffs in your everyday life, and they're all good ones.

Common Obstacles On The Road To Mastery

Once you commit to learning to dowse well, you will see progress, but the path to mastery is fraught with obstacles. These obstacles are opportunities, and they can be overcome. In this section we will discuss some of the most common ones and offer solutions.

The most common problem is the tendency to doubt your answers. Even though you think you entered the dowsing state, when you are new, you will doubt your answers. You'll wonder if you just made them up. The rational mind wants proof that your answer is correct, or at least that you were actually in a dowsing state, and it is natural to desire proof. But even when using the rational mind, you have to admit you often lack proof about the veracity of the conclusions your mind has come to. Often, you just have to act on them and see what happens. This is so much a part of everyday life that we don't question or even notice it. But doubt about dowsing will seem reasonable, because dowsing is a new activity for you, and you aren't sure of yourself.

We have found that it's easiest to overcome doubts about your dowsing answers if you dowse about simple but useful everyday situations that offer a chance for confirmation at some point. Like dowsing to find an open parking space in a large parking lot. Or choosing a menu item at a restaurant. Or picking a gift for a loved one.

Keeping a dowsing journal will make it a lot easier to chart progress. Write down your question and the answer you got and summarize what action you took. Date it and comment on your state of mind and other circumstances that you think might affect accuracy. Go back when you have verification and make notes about how accurate you felt the answer was. If the answer was way off, look hard at your question and see if it was too vague or short. If it was accurate, note that. Scan through your journal and notice how your confidence and accuracy grow. Because they will if you are using proper dowsing technique.

While doubt is something all new dowsers must learn to overcome, intermediate level dowsers will run into a different problem. When you have mastered dowsing for everyday activities and want to dowse about something really important, you might find that you just can't get into a dowsing state. What good is dowsing to you if you can't dowse about important things? This is the number one problem people have as they try to advance.

The usual problem is that although you can get into a dowsing state for everyday situations, you haven't mastered detachment, because you really aren't that attached to answers about things like where the best parking space is. When you decide to tackle more advanced topics, any attachment you have to answers will block you from getting into a dowsing state. You may find it easy to be curious about where the best parking space is, but when you want to know if your dog has cancer, that's a whole different ballgame.

This is not backsliding at all. You have mastered the basics, so now you have to master detachment. Detachment is required for entering the dowsing state. If you can't merely be a curious bystander when dowsing, you won't get into the dowsing state. So now you are going to have to master something new if you want to take your dowsing to the next level. How do you do that?

Fear and other strong emotions block your intuition. Your Inner Voice is quiet. Your mind must be still to access the information dowsing offers. Let's look at fear when you think about dowsing if your dog has cancer. They say fear stands for 'false evidence appearing real'. As such, fear is not useful at all to you. Unlike a gut feeling that tells you not to enter that dark alley, simple fear is not connected to any intuition. It's the rational mind telling you what MIGHT go wrong. But it is not the truth. It is just one bad scenario. And as you know, what you focus on expands, so you never want to focus on possible bad outcomes.

As an advanced dowser, you must detach yourself from which outcome you desire and simply desire to know the actual facts. There are therapies for releasing energies of negative emotions. We practice tapping regularly and have found it to be amazingly effective at helping us detach from particular worries about specific topics. The Emotion Code might be useful for this as well. Find a therapy that works for you, so that when you go back to the dowsing topic, you feel calmer and have no fear, no worry.

You see the pattern, don't you? Mastering dowsing forces you to change yourself, your outlook, your reactions. And it changes you in a positive way. Dowsing mastery is a path to great personal growth, even enlightenment, should that be a goal you have. It forces you to release judgment and negativity in order to get accurate answers. And that can only help you in your life.

Another obstacle we often hear about is when a person finds it very easy to dowse for others, even professionally, and get accurate answers, but when she wants to dowse for herself, she finds it difficult.

This is a variation on the detachment issue. When you are dowsing for a friend or client, you are more able to distance yourself from the answer in most cases than if you are dowsing for yourself about an important subject. As a professional, or even if you dowse often for friends, you will learn a level of detachment that will serve you well. But then, when you try to dowse for yourself, you will discover that it's different from dowsing for another person. You will need to develop a way to distance yourself and be curious, not attached to the answers.

Most often when this is the case, the person has been dowsing a lot for other people, way more than for herself. She perhaps dowses as part of her profession, and has little spare time or interest in dowsing for herself. She has mastered dowsing for others, and she thinks she should be just as competent to dowse for herself, but the sad truth is, she doesn't do it often. Dowsing for yourself is a special application. Our best advice is that you need to dowse for yourself often. Every day, if possible. Use the hints given above to master detachment and keep a journal of your efforts.

Remember to look at these challenges as opportunities. As you walk the path to mastery, sometimes it's uphill and sometimes it's downhill. You will become masterful as long as you keep going. Don't give up just because you run into a block of some kind. Obstacles are always a chance to take your skill to the next level.

Learn When Not To Dowse

There are times when you just shouldn't dowse, even if you are experienced. Do you know when those times are? And why is it that you shouldn't dowse at those times?

Knowing when NOT to dowse is just as important as developing your dowsing skill. If you dowse indiscriminately, you will run into issues that will make you think your dowsing is unreliable. But the fact is, often, when you try to dowse about something you shouldn't, you won't be able to get an accurate answer or your polarity will flip or you won't even be able to enter the dowsing state. This happens as a way to discourage you from dowsing, but unless you are clued in, you might just see it as a frustrating situation. And if this happens often enough, you might even give up dowsing.

There are some simple rules about when you should not dowse, and if you follow those, you will eliminate many instances of inaccurate and frustrating dowsing.

Never dowse when you have strong emotions or attachment to the answer

As we have covered in detail, you need to have a curious attitude when dowsing. If you want a particular answer or have strong emotions about the topic you are dowsing, don't dowse. You won't get an accurate answer. Work on yourself to release the attachment. If you cannot, then get a dowsing buddy or professional to dowse for you on that subject. As you master detachment, you will have fewer instances where you can't dowse, but even the most seasoned professional runs into this problem from time to time. Don't judge yourself. Just know when you aren't in a good place to dowse.

Always dowse ethically

We're actually dismayed at how few people understand the importance of dowsing ethics. Dowsing is an amazing power. You can abuse it, just as you can abuse any power. Think of dowsing as putting a listening device in someone's home and recording what is said. Or like a wiretap to eavesdrop on conversations. Or even a drone to follow someone somewhere.

Dowsing is a great tool for snoops and spies. You don't want to be either. It is unethical to pry into the private lives or intentions of other people. Never dowse about another person unless they tell you they want you to. Don't cheat by asking if you have permission using dowsing. That is a lame and illegitimate way to get permission. Ask them. If you are afraid to ask, it's probably because you know they won't say yes. So don't dowse about them. You accumulate negative karma if you violate dowsing ethics. It shows an unwillingness to respect boundaries and it is an abuse of power. It doesn't matter what your goal or excuse is, don't dowse about others unless they ask or give you verbal permission. As a side note, you want to be aware that like attracts like. If you do not respect the boundaries and privacy of others, you will find your own space being invaded. The golden rule applies.

Don't dowse about animals and properties you do not own unless the owner or caretaker has asked you to. It's the same as dowsing about people.

Our book *Dowsing Ethics* goes into the important topic of dowsing ethics in detail. We urge you to get a copy, because it contains useful exercises to help you form guidelines to follow when you dowse.

There are indeed some gray areas, but they are rare. It isn't appropriate to dowse about other people's intentions or the truth of what they are saying (as in someone on TV or someone you barely know). That's like wiretapping their phone. You don't have the right. However, if you are considering hiring a service person, like a mechanic, you have the right to dowse if what he said about you needing new brakes is true. But you had better be a good dowser, because your question could yield an incorrect answer. You always need to keep in mind that dowsing is not 100% accurate, and you should never judge or take action against someone solely based on a single dowsing. However, get another opinion on those brakes if your dowsing indicates the diagnosis is false.

Another acceptable situation with people you are close to and/or contemplating relationships of some kind with, is to dowse the compatibility of that relationship or person for your goals. It's a little easier to detach about a compatibility question than to ask if someone is lying about a business proposition or has real love for you. In relationships, it is always best to communicate verbally with someone rather than dowse about them behind their back. If you want to dowse to back up your feeling about accepting a marriage proposal, that's fine, but again, be aware dowsing isn't 100% accurate. It's wisest to have a dowsing buddy or professional check your answers. And remember never to use 'should' in dowsing questions, as in "Should I marry John?" The word 'should' implies a lot of stuff that will mess up your answers. To form good dowsing questions, be sure to get our book *Ask The Right Question,* which is mentioned in the Resources section.

Never dowse about things you can answer rationally

If you can look it up on Google, do so. Don't dowse. Dowsing is intended for answering questions you cannot answer rationally. If you use it for something you can find out rationally, like you're afraid to ask your boyfriend something, so you dowse about it instead, it's like using a hammer to loosen a bolt. When used for the wrong purpose, dowsing often yields wrong answers.

It's important to think about this subject so that you use dowsing as it should be used. This is not an ethical issue, and it won't create bad karma, but you'll get wrong answers and think you aren't a very good dowser, when in reality, it's just that you can get the answers in another way and they will be much more reliable.

Protocols For Entering The Dowsing State

We are definitely not going to say that if you follow a certain regimen, you will be guaranteed to be a great dowser. As with any skill, whether it is playing a sport or a musical instrument, you are the key factor. Yes, some folks have more innate 'talent,' but anyone can play an instrument or sports. Just some do better or learn faster. And we've all read stories or seen movies about people who didn't have talent (by other people's definition), but used raw will and action to compensate and became incredibly successful in their chosen field.

In this chapter, we've given you guideposts to help you find your way to the dowsing state. But we've also had requests from people, many of whom are interested in dowsing, but have monkey mind or limited time, who just plead with us to give them some type of routine to follow that might help them achieve the dowsing state if they practice it. The key phrase here being 'if they practice it.'

So in answer to those requests, we have put together a sample protocol. It won't work for everyone. It won't work at all if you don't do it regularly. But it is better than nothing, and it will probably help you with the aforementioned challenges. Be flexible and if necessary, adapt it to your needs and personality, keeping the key elements.

Please understand that doing this, especially if done in a rote fashion, does not promise success. But if you have the intention of mastering the dowsing state and becoming an accurate dowser, we believe practicing this routine will help you get there faster in many cases.

Most important is that you understand that no special routine is needed to dowse. You don't have to wash your pendulum, face North or ask your guides for protection. We want to dispel any mystery or feeling of 'magic' around dowsing other than the innate magic that is within you and allows you to tap into the answers you seek.

Don't get hung up on this routine and feel you cannot dowse without it. Please see this as a series of exercises to build your dowsing muscles. That's all. And eventually, you won't need these exercises. You'll know when. At that point, you'll find it easy to get into a dowsing state most of the time.

We're going to offer two protocols. The first will be for beginners and for those who have trouble stilling their mind. The second will assume you don't have too much trouble stilling the mind and will address dowsing more specifically. Try the first one, and if it's really simple, go on to the second. But if the first is challenging, continue to use it until you master it. We include suggestions in the next section of things we have used or think might also be helpful for training you to the dowsing state.

Protocol 1: Stilling the mind

Find a peaceful spot with no distractions; no people, no noise, nothing that will grab your attention. It is best to have a space that has positive and harmonious energy. Many people find it useful to create a special space in their home, like in a spare bedroom, for this purpose. Make the area clean, cheerful and if you like, decorate it with inspiring posters, use aromatherapy (frankincense is great) or do a space clearing periodically to insure the energy is supportive of your goals.

You might find it helpful to envision a tunnel of light in the doorway that strips you of any negative emotions and distractions as you enter the room.

Wear loose, comfortable clothing and sit in a very comfortable chair that supports your back well, one that you wouldn't mind sitting in for at least 5 minutes.

Close your eyes and try to keep them closed during the entire process.

Breathe deeply and slowly, not up in your chest, but in your belly. Focus on the in breath and the out breath. Try to make them long, but still comfortable. If any thoughts enter your mind, brush them away without judgment. Keep focused on breathing in and breathing out.

Notice any tension in your body. Start with your feet and relax the muscles in your feet while you continue to breathe deeply. Move up to your ankles, then your lower leg, doing the same thing. Just relaxing and breathing. Relax your thighs, buttocks and abdominal region. Then your chest. Continue breathing. Relax your back and shoulders and your arms, going down all the way to your fingers. Keep breathing and relax your neck. Feel a sense of heaviness as you relax.

Move your mouth, nose and squeeze your facial muscles a few times to soften them. Breathe deeply.

As distracting thoughts enter, brush them aside. Don't focus on them or run with them. Don't judge yourself. Let them go.

When you feel still, relaxed and clear, focus on one thing. It can be a color, like the color blue. Or a number. Or a scene that relaxes you. Pick just one thing to focus on and practice holding that in your mind for at least three minutes while you brush away any intruding thoughts. A timer may be used for this exercise. If you have problems with three minutes, start at one and increase the time as you master the technique.

When this exercise becomes easy for you, move on to the actual dowsing state protocol in the next exercise.

Protocol 2: Entering the dowsing state

This protocol assumes you have picked a topic you want to dowse, that you have clear goals and that you have created a very good dowsing question to ask once you get into a dowsing state. Please take our dowsing course and read our books on dowsing to help you with that part of the process.

This protocol also requires that you be self-aware and able to know when you are dowsing above your level of expertise. Following this protocol won't work if you are dowsing about something you are attached to. Work on detachment as needed before you do any dowsing.

Especially when you are new to dowsing, it is best to dowse in a quiet, harmonious place with no distractions. So follow the suggestions in Protocol 1 for setting up your dowsing space for success. As you master the dowsing state, you will be able to enter it even in a crowded, noisy location. But don't challenge yourself too much at first. Take it slowly.

Do this exercise without a dowsing tool. Deviceless dowsing is better for a number of reasons. Blink dowsing, which uses the response of your eyelids to give you the yes/no response or the body sway are two very good techniques that don't require a tool. If you aren't familiar with deviceless techniques, get our course or visit Discovering Dowsing for more information. See the Resource section for links. This book assumes you have had basic dowsing training. It is not a how-to-dowse book, so we won't go into detail on specific dowsing tools or techniques.

Repeat out loud or read your dowsing question several times (it is best to write your question down). As you say or read it, tune into the meaning of the words. Be aware of what you are trying to find out. Pull it into your being as you repeat it. Say it as often as it takes to really feel you 'own' the question.

Sit comfortably (or stand if you are doing the Body Sway). Close your eyes (or soft focus them if you are blink dowsing). Closing the eyes or soft focusing will help entrain the proper brain waves. Focusing on a tool will make it harder to get into the dowsing state.

Relax your body and breathe deeply, in your belly, not your chest.

Still your mind, brushing aside random thoughts without judgment until you feel you have cleared a space for your dowsing question. Be patient and take the time to reach this level of clarity before asking your question.

Ask the question (out loud or in your mind) one time only, focusing on it with all your attention so that the question is the only thing you are aware of. When you finish the question, hold that clear space inside as you wait for the answer with a curious and open attitude.

If you are new, the answer may come slowly. Almost everyone finds that if they practice, the answers begin to come more quickly, until eventually, you sometimes get the answer before you even finish asking the question. This is normal and a sign of mastery if you are in the dowsing state when it happens.

If you practice this protocol, you will find it easier and quicker to relax, clear your mind and focus on your question. Eventually, you won't need to rigidly follow a protocol. You will know how the dowsing state feels and how you feel when you fall out of it, and you will be able to summon it easily.

Someone watching you won't be able to see what's happening. It's all inside you. It's very subtle. But you will find being in the dowsing state gives you a sense of peace, a feeling of being fully in the moment and a lack of judgment or negative emotions.

Other Things That Might Help

Activities that may enhance your ability to reach the dowsing state

The research shows that the dowsing state is an altered brain state much like what is observed prior to paranormal activity, during healing and during states of higher consciousness, as observed in yogis. For that reason, it is logical to think that certain activities which play to those states could help you learn to enter a dowsing state faster and easier. In summary, anything that creates a dowsing state-like brain wave pattern is potentially helpful.

Here are some activities that might fit that description:

- Learn a healing method like Reiki or Jin Shin Jyutsu that is very simple and passive
- Meditate
- Use self-hypnosis on your personal growth topics
- Walk a labyrinth or use a finger labyrinth
- Use guided visualizations
- Learn another method of divination that taps into intuition, like tarot cards or a crystal ball

Behavior that can help improve your dowsing accuracy

Dowsing is a solitary pursuit for the most part. The more you practice, the better you will get. Especially if you use some tricks to help with your learning curve. The biggest help is to keep a dowsing journal. In your journal, you mark down date, describe your topic and frame of mind and record the exact question you used and what your answer was. Also note things like how strong the yes answer was, or how long it took to arrive, or what you felt at the time, like any particular sensations in your body. Maybe even give yourself a rating on a 0-10 scale for how detached you felt during the dowsing. Watch how the number changes over time. Note patterns in poor results and rework your questions to make them clearer.

Get a dowsing buddy. A second opinion is always a great idea, and having a dowsing buddy who will check your answers is very helpful. Dowsing is not 100% accurate, but when two people get the same exact answer to the same question, that's encouraging. Just don't tell your buddy what answer you got until she dowses for herself. A dowsing buddy is also someone to compare notes with, and your journal is a great resource for sharing your dowsing experiences.

Appeal to your senses

The sense of smell is the most ancient of senses, and certain essential oils have been proven to have an effect on higher states of consciousness. Sandalwood affects the pineal gland, which is connected to intuition and the third eye. Frankincense and myrrh affect the limbic system and were prized in ancient times higher than gold. The studies showed that dowsers' limbic systems were active during the dowsing state. So it might be worth diffusing or wearing some of these oils when dowsing.

Certain types of sound and music are said to have a powerful effect on brain state. If you have some New Age or spiritual music or tones that you want to experiment with, give them a try before you dowse to help you get into the dowsing state more easily.

Colors communicate with frequencies of their own. You might experiment with color in your special dowsing room. Blue, indigo and violet might be particularly suited for the dowsing state. But try different colors to focus on before you dowse and see what happens.

LISTEN to your Inner Voice

Dowsing is a way to reach for answers to specific questions, but your intuition is always there for you, whether you are asking or not. Learn to read the signs and hear your Inner Voice. Anything that helps you to tune into your intuition will also help improve your dowsing. At first, it may be hard to accept when information presents itself in a non-rational way. We all have this happen every day. You suddenly think about closing a certain window, but it doesn't make sense, so you ignore it. Later, during a sudden rainstorm, there is water damage to an antique desk near the window. If only you'd listened.

One thing that stops you from hearing your Inner Voice is multitasking and being hurried. Stop running around like a headless chicken. You have all the time in the world to do what you need to do, whether you are aware of it or not. Slow down and do one thing at a time. When you get a weird idea that pops in from nowhere, stop. Listen to it. Act on it. Even if it seems weird. The more you do this, the better your intuition becomes and the more it helps you. And the better your dowsing will get.

8

PITFALLS TO AVOID

Although we've mentioned pitfalls you face as you attempt to master the dowsing state, we wanted to put them all in one place so you can scan them from time to time and refresh your memory about how to overcome or avoid them. You are unique as a dowser. Some of these will be easy for you to deal with; others will be challenging. If you focus on becoming a masterful dowser, you will succeed. But be patient, as some of these can be very tricky.

Distractions

Most newbies or dowsers who don't dowse often will find distractions can totally derail the dowsing process, because you will find it hard to get into the dowsing state. So be sure to have a peaceful place to dowse while you are learning the basics. In time, you will be able to dowse with distractions. Some people are more subject to distractions than others, due to their personality.

Tiredness

Accessing your intuition with dowsing and getting into an altered state will also be challenging if you are tired. Don't try to dowse when you are mentally or physically exhausted. Do your best to get good sleep at night, as a rested body is vital for success in dowsing.

Dehydration

Most of your body is water, yet so few people drink enough water. When you are dehydrated, you are at risk for reversed polarity. Your body has polarity like a magnet, and when it flips, your yes/no answers also flip. Which means you think you got 'yes' for the answer, but it was really 'no.' We use a polarity check whenever we start a dowsing session, and sometimes during the session, to make sure our polarity has not flipped. A polarity question is an unambiguous question you know the answer to. We usually use our birthplace. If you dowse, "Was I born in _____(insert correct answer)," and the answer comes out 'yes,' then your polarity is fine. If you get 'no,' then you need to restore it. Take our course to learn more about dowsing pitfalls like polarity reversal.

Fear of being wrong and doubt about your answers

Doubt and fear are common emotions with new dowsers or those who dowse infrequently. Such emotions are normal as you begin honing any skill. The solution is to practice, improve your technique and gain confidence through success. There is no better way to do that than to get our course and read our books and practice a lot.

Attachment

When we use the word detachment, we are describing a state in which you are curious and not wedded to one particular answer. You cannot reach the dowsing state if you are attached to results. Detachment is a vital part of the dowsing state. Most people will find that it takes a lot of focus and practice to become detached, and that you learn quicker if you practice releasing judgment and attachment in your everyday life. Someone who has a strong belief about how things ought to be is going to find it more difficult to reach the dowsing state. This is another way that mastering dowsing can improve your life overall. We've all heard about 'going with the flow' and being 'nonjudgmental,' but how often do we really practice these things? If you practice releasing judgment and trusting the Universe in your everyday life, detachment will come to you quicker than if you do not.

Rational mind hijacks the process

If you have a monkey mind or have trained yourself to be very analytical and use your mind a lot, getting into the dowsing state will be more challenging, as the rational mind wants to be in control. Practicing meditation, guided visualization or self-hypnosis will help you learn to put the rational mind on hold for a while.

Ego

Everyone wants to say they aren't acting from ego, and some people will even try to tell you they have no ego. Wrong. Everyone has ego. You can't escape it. You can, however, set it aside when you are dowsing. If ego is in charge when you are dowsing, you will find that it's more important to you to be correct with your dowsing than to get the actual true answer. You will want to brag about your dowsing prowess. You will be eager to demonstrate how good a dowser you are. You'll be tempted to invade the privacy of others using dowsing. These aspects of ego will make it impossible to get into the dowsing state, as they prevent detachment. The ego is attached to results. You have to set it aside when dowsing.

. . .

Poor dowsing questions

Newbies often like to ask very short questions, in part because they don't understand a good question is often long and detailed, but also, because as newbies, they find it easier to focus on a short question. A dowsing question that doesn't include all the necessary parts will not yield a good answer. So even if you can access the dowsing state, you still need to master the other key factors in the technique. Taking our course and reading our book on dowsing questions will help you master this challenging part of the dowsing process.

Programmed questions are an exception to the rule of good questions being long, but since this isn't a dowsing course, we won't go into detail about that. Suffice it to say that if you create short programmed questions properly, they will be fine.

Skipping steps

Newbies or untrained dowsers will either intentionally or unintentionally skip vital steps in the dowsing process, thereby guaranteeing bad results. Every time you dowse, be patient and go through the necessary steps. If you skip crafting a good question, you are wasting your time. If you ignore the fact that you are upset and attached to the answer, you won't get an accurate response.

Dowsing when you shouldn't

Know when to dowse and when not to dowse. Everyone, even the most veteran dowsers, sometimes should not dowse about a subject. Dowsing is not something you should apply in all situations. Learn to discriminate appropriately.

Confusing dowsing with healing or energy transformation

Contrary to what some misinformed people are teaching, dowsing is simply a natural skill for getting answers to questions. It is not a healing or energy transformation technique, though the dowsing state itself may make it easier for you to do those things.

Being unwilling to learn and grow

Because dowsing is often portrayed as something psychic rather than a learned skill, many people approach dowsing as if they expect they don't have to study, practice or grow into a masterful dowser. This attitude keeps them from mastering dowsing. The dowsing state is not your natural brain state. It is an altered state you need to learn. If you will approach dowsing as a skill and not be afraid to face up to mistakes and weaknesses, you will learn to overcome them, and you will become masterful.

Thinking dowsing is always correct

Dowsing is a human skill. All skills can be exercised masterfully, but even masters make mistakes. That's part of being human. Never assume dowsing is 100% accurate. That is one reason we say it isn't ethical to dowse about another person without their permission. Even if it were ethical to do so, dowsing is not always right, and how could you justify taking action or judging someone based something that is not infallible?

Failure to practice

Laziness is inherent to humans to keep them from wasting energy unnecessarily. Practicing can seem boring and repetitious. You may feel you are not making fast enough progress. We all live busy lives, and taking time to practice and master a skill is a real commitment.

Just like getting into an exercise program or learning t'ai chi or becoming good at playing piano, becoming a masterful dowser takes time and effort. The dowsing state is not the natural human brain state. You will need to master it. If you commit the time and effort, you will succeed. And it will pay you back many times over.

9

SUMMARY

We hope that you have arrived at this page after reading the entire book. If you skipped to this section hoping to save yourself the trouble of reading the whole book, naughty, naughty! Go back and read.

As you now know, the dowsing state is a very complex and difficult subject to understand and to teach, which is why it has not been taught well in the past. It's challenging to master it using only what you learn in a book, but we hope that we have provided a lot of good ideas and methods that will help you with this fundamental step towards success.

The first and most important takeaway from this book is that if you are not in the dowsing state, you are not dowsing. A tool can move whether you are actually dowsing or not. You can get an answer whether you are in the dowsing state or not. But if you are not in the dowsing state, then you are not dowsing, and the answer is not reliable. This is not something we have decreed; it is the very definition of dowsing.

It is really hard for some people to accept this fact, because they either have not had good dowsing training or they misunderstand what dowsing is. Dowsing is not a psychic ability, so you can't just pick up a pendulum and expect to be a great dowser. Dowsing is a natural skill, but a skill, nonetheless. It's far more natural than playing a piano or doing a high dive properly. It's even more natural than riding a horse. But like all of those, it is a skill. A skill is something that requires mastery of proper technique for success. Without proper dowsing training, you probably don't have good technique. And that means your accuracy will be poor.

It's annoying to think that mastering dowsing is like learning to play a musical instrument. Who wants to practice all the time? We all want to jump to the exciting questions and answers, but that's like expecting to play "Moonlight Sonata" without any piano lessons. Only a very rare prodigy could do that. And most of us are not prodigies. But the good news is that anyone can learn to dowse and can master the dowsing state with practice.

It is very easy to be misled about what dowsing is because of the emphasis on tool use and the movement of the tool apparently giving the answer. The tool does not give you the answer. The tool is a crutch, a way of amplifying your body's reaction so that you can more easily see the answer. We advocate mastering deviceless dowsing for a number of reasons. One is that you will more quickly learn to recognize your body's "yes" and "no" responses that way, and another is because focus on the tool gives wrong impressions and creates bad habits, leading to the common misperception of dowsing tool as magic wand. We've even seen people who can't dowse if they don't have their pendulums. A tool is not required for dowsing, and indeed, studies show that deviceless dowsing is more likely to be a coherent brain wave state using all four brain waves: alpha, beta, theta and delta.

The dowsing state has not been fully studied, but preliminary research shows that it is an altered brain state measurable using EEG devices. Thus the dowsing state is dramatically different from the normal waking state, because instead of having just one type of brain wave, there are four coherent and active during the dowsing state. We cannot emphasize the importance of this enough. You must be in an altered state to dowse. You can't just swing a pendulum and get an answer.

Unfortunately, it takes time and practice to get a 'feel' for the dowsing state, because it is so subtle. It is often easier to recognize when you are not in a dowsing state as opposed to when you are in a dowsing state. The dowsing state does not feel like when the brain is totally in alpha or beta mode. There is no place for fear or other negative emotions. The mind is still and clear. Your focus is 100% on your good dowsing question, and you are open and ready to accept whatever the answer is, because you are curious, not attached. So if any of those conditions are not present, you are not in a dowsing state. Most people are readily able to detect the lack of these conditions, and that's a good place to start.

The dowsing state is akin in some ways to meditation, but includes two more coherent brain wave patterns than found in meditation. It is more like the patterns you see at the onset of paranormal phenomena, a higher level of consciousness and healing.

We feel that the dowsing state is not unique to dowsing, that it is shared by these conditions and states, and perhaps should have a broader name that would include all of these activities, but comprehensive research will need to be done to verify this theory. It is not surprising to us that truly committed, masterful dowsers are often also very involved in either healing of some type or a commitment to experiencing higher levels of consciousness or have some paranormal talents, even if you just call an amazing ability to manifest positive outcomes a paranormal talent.

While it would be easy to be discouraged when you learn that the dowsing state is so challenging to talk about and master, we urge you not to give up on dowsing. You can learn to be a great dowser. There are so many wonderful benefits to dowsing mastery, and if you commit to becoming masterful, you will reap those benefits. We've written a lot of books on dowsing to help you along your path. We also created the best courses possible. We encourage you to read our other books and take our course, as they will help you master dowsing and figure out how to apply it throughout your life. See the Resources section for details on your next step towards dowsing mastery.

Happy Dowsing!

10

RESOURCES

Dowsing is a natural skill that involves technique, and the dowsing state is the most vital part, but it is still only one step. If you want to master dowsing, we'd like to help you. We have lots of resources you can use.

Learn Dowsing Technique & Applications

Free Help: Enjoy 200 pages of free articles, videos and recorded presentations on our free website Discovering Dowsing at www.discoveringdowsing.com.

Join Our Online Community: If you are passionate about using dowsing and intuition to improve your life, join our Discovering Dowsing course online community, where one fee gives you lifetime access to our Basic, Advanced and Postgraduate courses in dowsing plus articles and exercises about intuition. The Discovering Dowsing course is the ideal, private place to interact with like-minded people. www.discoveringdowsingcourse.com

Read our dowsing books

You can visit Sixth Sense Books and register to get notification of new books and discounts and choose up to four free ebooks when you register, at www.sixthsensebooks.com.

Bibliography

Stillman, Ed. "Dowsers' Brainwave Characteristics." *The American Dowser.* Winter 1997: 6-18. Print.

Stillman, Ed. "Dowsers' Brainwave Characteristics, Part 2. Brainwave Coherence and Delta Waves." *The American Dowser.* Spring 1998: 9-26. Print.

Dispenza, Dr. Joe. *You Are The Placebo.* Carlsbad: Hay House, 2014. Print.

Fannin, Jeffrey L., Ph.D. *Understanding Brainwaves.* http://drjoedispenza.com/files/understanding-brainwaves_white_paper.pdf

PLEASE LEAVE A REVIEW

Our goal was to introduce you to a key aspect of the dowsing process and dispel misconceptions about this natural skill, so that you can become a confident, accurate dowser.

Your review will help other readers to decide if this book is for them. Please go to the site where you bought this book and leave as detailed a review as possible. Thanks!

ABOUT THE AUTHORS

Nigel and Maggie Percy of Sixth Sense Solutions have been dowsing since the 1990's, and in 2001 set up their company, which focused on teaching dowsing and offering services on the internet globally. In 2017, they shifted their focus to writing books and developing the Discovering Dowsing site for dowsers. See their books at Sixth Sense Books and their fiction author sites.

For more information
www.discoveringdowsing.com
support@discoveringdowsing.com

Made in the USA
Las Vegas, NV
17 January 2022